The Prettiest Love Letters
in the World

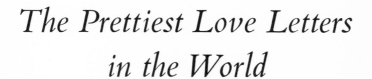

The Prettiest Love Letters
in the World

Letters between
LUCREZIA BORGIA
& PIETRO BEMBO
1503 to 1519

Translation and Preface
HUGH SHANKLAND
Wood engravings
RICHARD SHIRLEY SMITH

COLLINS HARVILL
8 Grafton Street   London W1
1987

William Collins Sons and Co. Ltd
London   Glasgow   Sydney   Auckland
Toronto   Johannesburg

BRITISH LIBRARY CATALOGUING IN PUBLICATION DATA

The prettiest love letters in the world
1 Bembo, Pietro — Biography   2 Authors, Italian —
16th century — Biography   3 Borgia, Lucrezia, *Duchess*
of Ferrara   4 Papal States — Nobility — Biography
858'.309   PQ4608

ISBN   0 00 272047 7

First published in a limited edition as *Messer Pietro Mio* by Libanus Press 1985
This edition first published by Collins Harvill 1987
© Hugh Shankland and Libanus Press 1985, 1987

Handset in 14 pt Monotype Bembo

Made and printed in the United States of America

The Prettiest Love Letters
in the World

PREFACE

POPULAR HISTORY's chamber of horrors will no doubt forever feature a chilling waxwork of Lucrezia Borgia as the World's Most Wicked Lady although modern historians have long since separated fact from fiction, dismissing as preposterous or unproven all the monstrous acts which were attributed to Lucrezia by anti-Borgia publicists in her lifetime and later reworked with such relish by the nineteenth century's trembling worshippers of Belles Dames Sans Merci. Flatterers writing under Borgia protection were fond of proclaiming Lucrezia in every way worthy of her classical namesake (not so silly when one recalls that 'Lucrece the chaste' was no virgin herself and similarly blessed with good looks and a very high position in society) but did not draw the less favourable parallel that in one sense or another both women had to endure male enforcement. Lucrezia Borgia underwent three marriages in submission to the political and dynastic drives of the men who ruled her family. From adolescence until the Borgias' sudden eclipse when she was barely twenty-three her career was determined by two exceptionally forceful men: her own Holy Father, Pope Alexander VI, a brilliant and winning man of the world of whom Machiavelli wrote not without esteem that he 'never did or thought of anything but deceiving people', and Cesare Borgia, her dynamic and boundlessly ambitious elder brother.

Lucrezia was born in 1480, the sixth child of Cardinal Rodrigo Borgia and his third by his Roman mistress Vanozza de' Cattaneis.

Rodrigo had owed his cardinalate at the age of twenty-five to his uncle Alonso de Borja, Pope Calixtus III (1455-8), but entirely due to his own abilities he held the second highest office in the Church, that of Vice-Chancellor, for over thirty-five years before obtaining the Papacy itself. When elected in 1492, the year of Columbus and the fall of Grenada, he dropped all plans for marrying his favourite daughter higher into the aristocracy of his native Spain, choosing to reserve her as a useful card to strengthen his hand in the precarious world of Italian politics. She was no more than thirteen when he had her married to the widowed ruler of Pesaro, Giovanni Sforza, a papal commander who was distantly related to Ludovico Sforza, the powerful ruler of Milan. Lucrezia tried to be a good wife, but it was a loveless marriage. When she was seventeen and it became clear to her father that Sforza was an ineffectual soldier and probably also double-crossing him, the Pope used his office to force a divorce on the debatable grounds that the marriage had never been consummated. Understandably Sforza resented this public denial of his potency, and in revenge spread the scandalous story (germ of the Lucrezia legend) that Pope Alexander wished to reserve his daughter for his own pleasure. Another damaging story, for which there is no solid evidence at all, is that while Borgia partisans were trying to convince the College of Cardinals of Lucrezia's virginity she had a secret affair with a young Spaniard in Vatican service and eventually gave birth to his child while hidden from the public eye in a Roman convent. All that is certain is that the young man whom rumour named was soon no more capable of hindering her family's plans for her future than any other corpse in the Tiber. In 1498 she was married to Alfonso, Duke of Bisceglie and Prince of Salerno, a slight step up the ladder since this eighteen-year-old boy was a bastard son of Alfonso II of Aragon, the late King of Naples. The intention was to improve the Neapolitan connection further by marrying Cesare Borgia to the new King's daughter, but when this scheme met resistance the Pope turned his attention to France, a long-standing opponent of Aragonese power in Italy. Cesare Borgia secured for wife the sister of the King of Navarre and while in France prepared a Franco-papal strategy that was to be the doom of Lucrezia's second marriage. Reliable reports say that she and her gentle-natured husband were happy; there was an early miscarriage, then in November 1499 came a son who was christened Rodrigo after his formidable grandfather. But in the previous month Louis XII of France had invaded Italy, seizing Milan and reasserting his claim to Naples. The Borgias, father and son, stepped up their courtship of the man of the moment and disregarding earlier promises to the Aragonese pledged support for Louis' proposed campaign against Naples in exchange for French aid for their own schemes to gain control in Central Italy. With Louis' blessing and a detachment of French troops Cesare set about carving out a state for himself in Romagna by ousting the mainly unpopular local lords, semi-independent vassals of the Church. Precisely what led to the murder of Lucrezia's second husband on 18 August 1500 is not clear, but undoubtedly this fruitful collaboration with the French made her marriage link with Naples now seem a wasted investment. On that day, with the excuse of a suspected Aragonese conspiracy and undeniably at Cesare's command, Alfonso Bisceglie was strangled in the couple's Vatican apartment, despite Lucrezia's frantic efforts to save him. The victim and his widow were both just twenty years old. Lucrezia's unbroken sobs so irritated her father that after a fortnight he had her sent away from Rome to get over her grief out of earshot.

Such, before Lucrezia's arrival in Ferrara for her final marriage, were her principal 'adversities' to which Pietro Bembo so pointedly alludes in some of these letters. The precise effect upon her of such violent events is hard to determine, but even after the shock of Alfonso's death her allegiance to her family was never really in doubt. She was soon reconciled with her brother and when she came back to Rome she was still young, and once again the little idol of the Vatican. According to one report, in an unusual mood of defiance she complained to her father that her husbands had been 'very unlucky' and that she would never remarry, but other accounts of Lucrezia when she was again the subject of marriage speculation seldom fail to note her gay spirits and captivating smile. So scant is the record of her feelings that it is difficult to decide whether this recovered poise was the mark of a basically light-hearted nature or the plucky defence of a hurt and secretive young woman. Niccolò Cagnolo of Parma, about a year before she met Pietro Bembo, described her appeal: 'She is of medium height and slender build; her face is oval, the nose is well formed; her hair is golden, her eyes tawny; the mouth is full and large with the whitest teeth; her throat is smooth and white yet becomingly full. She is all good humour and gaiety.'

Her brother's successes in Romagna and the enormous wealth which he and his father were amassing by fair means and foul had made it possible to negotiate a far more prestigious marriage than before. Within months another Alfonso had been selected for her: Alfonso d'Este, eldest son of Ercole d'Este, the Duke of Ferrara. To Lucrezia, who possessed the true Borgia presence and delight in self-display, this latest political deal promised entry to an old and illustrious Italian dynasty and the highest position for a woman in one of the most glittering courts in Italy; it might also bring greater security, for as long as her future remained tied solely to the ambitions of her own family it was only too evident that she would have little real control over her life. The importance of the marriage to Borgia strategy was obvious to everyone. The territories of the Duchy of Ferrara, which stretched from the Appennines to the Adriatic along the fertile plain of the Po, lay between Romagna and the Veneto; rich and well-defended Ferrara was a papal vicariate and by long tradition anti-Venetian; to yoke the white eagle of Este with the

Borgia bull would profitably extend the family's influence and dynastic prospects and also provide Cesare's expanding 'Duchy of Romagna' with a friendly northern buttress against attack from the hostile Republic of Venice, the most powerful of the Italian states. Despite his son's protests and his own considerable misgivings Ercole d'Este eventually capitulated to the Borgias' bullying pleas, and French pressure. But he drove a hard bargain in return, demanding an unprecedented dowry of 200,000 ducats and guarantees of lucrative papal exemptions and privileges for the Duchy and for members and favourites of the house of Este. Under such purely political and mercenary circumstances it is not hard to appreciate that once Lucrezia was beyond her father's immediate protection she would need unusual resources of courage and charm if ever she hoped to win Ferrarese esteem, let alone affection.

On 2 February 1502, after a spectacular month-long journey by way of the newly-conquered territories carefully stage-managed by Alexander and Cesare, Lucrezia made her triumphal entry into Ferrara with a 700-strong company of Roman and Spanish gentlemen, prelates, ladies-in-waiting, men-at-arms, servants, craftsmen, cooks and entertainers. But hardly had the memorable wedding week of banquets and interminable musical and theatrical evenings come to an end when the grim old Duke, who had ruled Ferrara severely and thriftily for thirty years, took steps to send the unpopular 'Spaniards' packing and to curb Lucrezia's extravagances. With no support from her new husband Lucrezia fought hard against these impositions, eventually winning some concessions over her allowance and managing to retain a number of attendants, including her three celebrated Spanish buffoons; her wildly flirtatious cousin Angela Borgia stayed behind, and so did some other favourite ladies-in-waiting.

The first year of adaptation to Ferrara was particularly lonely and difficult. According to the code of the time she had been unable to bring little Rodrigo with her, the child of the tragic second marriage. In the vast moated Este castle at the centre of the city she was given a three-room apartment which overlooked a garden, the bedchamber later being connected by passageway with Alfonso's rooms. To sophisticated courtiers her new husband seemed uncouth. Don Alfonso's physique was sturdy, and his appetites pretty coarse; he had little patience with the pomp and circumstance of court life, and scant interest in letters and learning. Although he shared the Este pleasure in music and the theatre he was more notoriously fond of whores and war-machines, and like many another princely hedonist of his time had a touch of the pox. His considerable talents were practical; he played the viol with skill, enjoyed work at the lathe and the potter's wheel, and pursued his obsession with artillery to the point of learning to cast his own cannon. As Duke, and eventually one of the foremost generals of Italy, his personal device was to be a fiery bombshell. In a famous portrait in later years Titian painted him as a powerful and wary figure: thickly bearded, hawk-nosed, steady eyes on his adversary's moves, one hand by the hilt of his sword, the other fingering the cold iron mouth of a huge cannon. When he reluctantly married Lucrezia he was twenty-six and already a widower, his first wife, a Sforza, having died in childbirth. Of course in such a marriage of political convenience husband and wife were hardly expected to fall in love, however Alfonso seems to have generally displayed a cool yet correct respect for his wife and later appreciated Lucrezia's administrative abilities to the extent of entrusting state business to her and his brother Cardinal Ippolito in his absence. In bed, as first despatches informed her delighted father, Don Alfonso performed with promising gusto, and by day amused himself with other women. Though he affected indifference to Lucrezia's circle and her literary friends he could be a suspicious husband, and no doubt had his reasons. According to legend when Lucrezia was shown round the castle she was made to look long at the spot where an earlier Este Duke had caused his own son and his Duchess by second marriage to be beheaded for their misconduct together. The four sons of Ercole d'Este were violent men. In 1505 Cardinal Ippolito was to have his brother Giulio set upon and nearly blinded because, so it is said, Angela Borgia declared Ippolito's whole body was not worth Don Giulio's dark eyes; and when this attack spurred Don Giulio to plot with Don Ferrante to kill Alfonso and Ippolito and seize the throne, Alfonso, who was by then Duke, had his two brothers shut up for life in the family castle. Este rule over Ferrara was absolute and despotic, squeezing an overtaxed and discontented people to pay for their luxurious life and to maintain the nobles and bankers and merchants whose loyalty to the Este was guaranteed by lucrative privileges and the sale of influential public offices, and by the social attractions and rich pageantry of court life.

Despite her early difficulties Lucrezia soon came into her own as the presiding female presence in Ferrara, and already during that first year, since her father-in-law the Duke was a widower, she was formally termed 'la Duchessa'. Her youthful sophistication, her wild Spanish dancing, her pretty girls-in-waiting, her fascinating past and powerful connections, began to attract a lively little court within the greater one. Poets and scholars, normally the most impoverished of courtiers, were in particular drawn to a rich and easily flattered patroness. Antonio Tebaldeo, famous in the courts of Italy for his eccentric brand of Petrarchan verse, became a trusted friend and in time her personal secretary. Lodovico Ariosto, the future author of the *Orlando furioso*, had written a Latin epithalamium for her union with Alfonso and according to Bembo became genuinely 'inflamed' by her 'surpassing qualities' (XII). A wealthy and influential pair of Latinists, Tito and Ercole Strozzi, father and son, vied to turn out extravagant lines extolling her matchless beauty and supreme intelligence. This was the small coterie of like-minded courtiers which was soon to welcome Pietro Bembo. And in good time Bembo himself would also produce a Latin encomium for Lucrezia; reading between the lines of its obligatory hyperbole, one realises that apart from her exceptional flair for dancing Lucrezia had little more than the normal social accomplishments of girls of her station: tolerable on the lute, delightful when declaiming Petrarch, and capable herself (though there now exists no other evidence for it) of turning out a passable verse or two. Brought up between the cultures of Spain and Italy, Lucrezia was a good linguist however, speaking Catalan and Castilian and Italian, and quite familiar with Latin; and later she also acquired good French and a little Greek. Bembo, who was ten years older than her, enjoyed playing the role of amorous preceptor to a brilliant pupil but in comparison to his wide learning her own was only one-chapter-deep, as is indicated by the fact that to Ferrara along with the caskets of jewellery and scores of dresses she brought a tiny library of less than a dozen books which included nothing more scholarly than Petrarch's *Rime* and a book of Spanish love poetry.

Her first obligation was of course to provide a male heir for the house of Este. She was with child almost at once, but it was a difficult pregnancy and during the hot summer in low-lying Ferrara she contracted her first and nearly fatal attack of malarial fever. The men of the family, fearing the worst, revealed the degree of their anxiety by the level of their menaces. Cesare ordered his best physician to Ferrara and then himself donned disguise and turned up dramatically at her bedside. Her father wrote to Ercole d'Este implying that the future of his Duchy depended on whether or not the doctors were able to save Lucrezia. In September she gave birth to a still-born premature daughter, but soon began to recover and retired for a while to the convent of Corpus Domini. She was still wearing flattering black when one month later Ercole Strozzi informed her that his good friend Pietro Bembo, the Venetian scholar and poet, had come to reside on Ferrarese territory.

PIETRO BEMBO was no stranger to Ferrara. His father Bernardo Bembo, a leading Venetian patrician of great classical erudition, former ambassador to Florence and Rome, had been appointed in 1497 'Visdomino' or co-ruler in Ferrara, a deeply unpopular office re-imposed on the Ferrarese after Venetian supremacy in the most recent war between the neighbouring states. Pietro, then studying philosophy at Padua University, had duly joined his father and attended the University in Ferrara where he studied under Nicolò Leoniceno, one of the most celebrated humanist educators of the time. The Venetian senator had hoped that the experience of court life would assist his son in preparing for a similar career as a senior public servant and diplomat but Pietro was attracted to this world of privileged make-believe for other reasons, finding it more congenial to his temperament than what he judged to be the cold manners and mercantile priorities of Venetian public life. His lean good looks and well-bred demeanour and breadth of culture made him popular at a court where writers and scholars enjoyed some notoriety and the learned Duke's attention. When his father's term of office expired Pietro stayed on for a while to savour the sweet advantages of princely patronage; Ercole d'Este, impressed by the young man's scholarship and doubtless also making a painless gesture of goodwill towards Venice, had provided him with the freedom to study and write at leisure in the sumptuous Este summer residence at Belriguardo. More recently Pietro had been seen in Ferrara on fleeting visits to contact a married Venetian woman, Maria Savorgnan, with whom he was conducting a secret affair.

In Ferrara Bembo's closest friend was Ercole Strozzi, the gifted young author of fluent Latin epigrams and elegiacs, whose father was himself a Latin poet of more than local renown and also, as supreme magistrate of the Duchy, one of the richest and most hated magnates in the land. Time and again we find 'Messer Ercole' mentioned in the correspondence between Bembo and Lucrezia, and this dashing 'cripple Strozzi' exercises considerable fascination. He cut an unusual figure at court, dressing with an extravagant flair that astounded even the fashion-conscious Ferrarese, and yet a paralysed misshapen leg forced him to use crutches. Ercole, who had several illegitimate children, was an impulsive womaniser (Vulcan was bandy-legged, he used to quip, but that did not deter Venus) and his career shows that he had nothing less than a vocation for amorous intrigue. Maria Savorgnan and Bembo had already counted on his assistance during their illicit affair, while in the friendship between Bembo and Lucrezia he was to play the part of the most accomplished go-between, skills he was again called upon to use a few years later during Lucrezia's highly hazardous intrigue with the Marquis of Mantua. In age Bembo and Strozzi were very close, both in their early thirties in 1502, and they had much else in common. Both men were first-born sons of high-ranking families whose fathers were leading figures in their countries' affairs, and from these well-lettered patriarchs both had acquired exceptional aptitude for classical studies; both were accomplished poets who did not separate the pursuit of letters from the pursuit of ladies, each taking a lively interest in the other's adventures, and each with a gift for moderating sensuality with wit which made them admirably suited to the refined gallantries of court life. There were differences too: Strozzi's natural place was at court, at the centre of influence and intrigue, whereas Bembo in spite of all his urbanity had a genuine need for the studious quiet he created for himself in the countryside. He wrote masterly Latin and Greek but held Italian to be a noble language too, while Strozzi affected an aristocratic disdain for the vulgar tongue. Strozzi had money to burn, and did, but Bembo, conscious of his degree of dependence on his father, could not allow himself the same debonair extravagance. His friend's manner was edged with malice and a teasing arrogance which could be thrilling to women but less endearing to men, and as a public magistrate he was to prove as ruthless and unpopular as his father, while Bembo's nature was much more mild and conciliatory, with even a tinge of well-bred melancholy. 'Messer Pietro' had the gift of forming enduring friendships and in a long life in which he attained great eminence in Italian political and cultural life he was almost universally respected and admired, but Messer Ercole was to meet his death at the age of thirty-five, the victim of a brutal assassination that has never been satisfactorily explained, partly because it suited so many people.

In Venice in the summer of 1502 Bembo received a visit from Strozzi who was in the city to see a 'cruel woman' for whom he had had a long admiration, and also to buy precious additions to Lucrezia's wardrobe. Ercole, we may safely assume, gave his friend all the latest gossip from Ferrara, and they probably also discussed their current literary projects. Ercole was writing a spate of verses celebrating Lucrezia and the glories of the Borgia, and also planned something on a larger scale in her honour. The exuberant flattery of his verses, his extravagant presents and genuine appreciation of the difficulties of her life in Ferrara had quickly won Lucrezia's trust. He was probably the liveliest member of her company and the political influence he wielded in Ferrara was invaluable to her; moreover his expensive taste and rich imagination in matters of dress were great assets for a young woman who was already resolved to rival the reputation of Isabella d'Este, her hostile sister-in-law, as the most fashionable lady in Italy. As for Bembo, he was now a leading member of the circle of classical scholars which his old friend Aldus Manutius, the famous scholar-printer, had gathered about him in Venice; recently he had given Aldus editorial assistance with a new series of popular editions in italic type, initiating a very successful run of Italian works with his carefully corrected text of Petrarch's *Rime* Bembo's reputation as a Latinist was based on some well-turned verse and a lively dialogue about his ascent of Mount Etna while a student of Greek in Messina. This *De Aetna*, beautifully printed by Aldus in 1495 in Francesco Griffo's first Roman fount, has earned from bibliophiles the unique tribute of 'the first modern book' and is also the ultimate source of the Monotype Bembo in which the main text of the book in your hand is cast. Closest to Bembo's heart at this time was the manuscript of a work of Italian prose and verse which, when finally published three years later, was to be dedicated to Lucrezia Borgia herself. This is his famous *Gli Asolani*, a Platonic-cum-Petrarchan treatise on the torments and joys and heavenly rewards of men's love for women, and it was destined to make a considerable impression on the culture of his time. It takes the form of a friendly dispute about love between three handsome young Venetian gentleman-poets and three comely young ladies temporarily relieved of their husbands, all seated together on fresh grass among shady trees in the palace gardens at Asolo in the green Euganean hills, and were it not for its often over-fastidious tone it would be the perfect complement to the contemporary art of Giorgione. Bembo, who grew up speaking the vernacular of Venice, had composed it in an exquisitely revived archaic Tuscan derived from Boccaccio and Petrarch, but even after labouring for five years he did not feel ready for publication. Extreme preoccupation with form (in every sense) was deeply characteristic of this man who in these years was already beginning to evolve his aesthetic of a decorous *aurea mediocritas*, art and manners trimmed of vulgar or rhetorical or even vital excess, in which resides the best and the worst of all he taught the Renaissance in Italy and Europe.

In the minor art of penning memorable love-letters – small works of the heart written with a little too much craft to be thrown away without feeling that posterity could be missing something – Pietro Bembo had served a full apprenticeship. Though nothing remains of any letters to 'M.G.', his first love, almost the entire correspondence with his second great flame, Maria Savorgnan, was preserved by him and then (like the letters to Lucrezia) revised and reserved for publication upon his death. The many letters he wrote in 1500 and 1501 to Maria (a very lively and talented woman as her own side of the correspondence proves) reveal a very genuine respect for women and an equally strong need for female attention and sympathy; but just as obviously they betray a self-gratifying temptation to turn life into literature, so that each letter is at once about the power of love and the lover's power with words. Petrarch, 'the enamoured Tuscan', presided over all his early liaisons, like a tender learned Cupid. Two years later, when it came to 'consigning himself to the flames for the third time' (XV) and it was Lucrezia's turn to be the first to read his love letters, the affectations and emotional tactics are often the same, identical quotations from Petrarch appear, even the appeals to his 'other half' and the 'crystal heart', but these letters are marked by a new restraint that must make some of them masterpieces in this long outdated but once living and respected genre. The lachrymose self-indulgence of the earlier letters is severely curbed, the touch is both lighter and more assured. Style was everything to Bembo, who always scrupulously revised and refined his writings, including his correspondence. More than the intuitive accuracy of a true poet, he had the impeccable precision of a humane philologist, and all his work lies midway between invention and convention, modulated passion, sweet reason. The letters to Lucrezia, because they were un-doubtedly born of genuine passion but one which needed to be care-fully controlled by force of circumstances, show the best of Bembo, idealisation rather than mere standardisation of thought and feeling. Nonetheless, however much he may have revised them later, one feels that even as he wrote these letters he was conscious of producing models of love-prose. Indeed Bembo's epistolary experience played an important part in the evolution of *Gli Asolani* in which he was carefully organising his life and his reading, his ideal loves and his literary ideals, for a larger public. Begun when he was captivated by 'M.G.', mostly written during the years of Maria Savorgnan, finally dedicated to Lucrezia, *Gli Asolani* commemorates the three loves of his youth.

Bembo had allowed the manuscript to circulate among friends whom he knew to be in sympathy with his aims, but he was nervous of publication because he realised the work would be looked upon as an undignified venture into the vernacular for one who moved in the sort of scholarly circles where contributions to knowledge or literature were only made in Latin or Greek, and whose prospects of a career as a senior public servant would not be helped by what many of his father's colleagues would have condemned as very frivolous matter. Evidently he was already regarded with some diffidence since in spite of his father's eminence he had three times been overwhelmingly outvoted when competing for high offices in the state. There is no doubt that these humiliations strengthened his ambition to make his way by the pen, if necessary far from Venice. He had formed no deep attachments since winding up the affair with Maria Savorgnan, and when Ercole Strozzi encouraged him to return to Ferrara, and his devoted brother Carlo offered to help look after his interests in Venice, there seemed no reason to stay.

On 14 October 1502 he installed himself in the capacious Strozzi villa in the hamlet of Ostellato on the shores of Lake Comacchio, about twenty-five miles downstream from Ferrara. At Ostellato, which he knew well from earlier days, there was the cultured company of the elder Strozzi, now nearly an octogenarian, and of his lively son when he could spare a day or two away from town. Hunting and fishing parties called occasionally and tried to persuade him out, but otherwise he had more or less to himself the big turreted house with its spacious rooms, the family library, the gardens, and the wide views of trees and water. Cola Bruno, his faithful secretary, arrived with his books and his dog Bembino, conveyed to him by boat over the Venetian lagoon and the intricate waterways of Comacchio. He would be up early and would read and write through most of the day. On occasions he went into Ferrara where he kept lodgings. And before long he met Lucrezia, playing host to her and her company during an outing in mid-November when they made a surprise call at the villa before returning upstream to Ferrara. The next day he wrote to Ercole that he would have preferred to entertain much longer 'such a beautiful and elegant woman who is not superstitious about anything'.

Winter was the great festive season at the Italian courts and Bembo was often a guest at the palace receptions, tournaments, concert parties, theatrical evenings, masked balls and intimate suppers which filled the calendar until Lent. In Palazzo Strozzi Ercole threw a spectacular new year's ball in Lucrezia's honour, and on 15 January Pietro boasted in a letter to his brother in Venice that he had received 'honours and compliments in plenty' from the Duchessa. 'Every day,' he wrote, 'I find her a still worthier lady, seeing she has far excelled all my expectations, great though they were after hearing reports of her from so many lips, and most of all from Messer Ercole'. Two years later, in his last long love-letter to Lucrezia (XXX) he was to claim he had fallen in love at first sight and only circumstances had compelled him to hide his feelings. No doubt he was struck by her at once, and flattered by her attention, but he could scarcely yet dare admit he might fall seriously in love with her and still less she with him. Her rank and her sex demanded amorous homage, just as she was expected gracefully to acknowledge men's respectful attentions. Besides, she was surrounded by several very pretty and less risky propositions, such as young Angela Borgia, or the vivacious Sienese girls, Nicola and Lisabetta, perhaps the very same trio of nymphs whom he and Strozzi in their correspondence fondly referred to as Polyxena, Cinthia & Clymene.

Lent saw Pietro back in his retreat in Ostellato, resolved to work hard through the spring and summer. Ercole kept him in touch with events in Ferrara, supplying him especially with reports of Lucrezia.

'Lucretian letters', Pietro termed them. His speculations were tantalisingly aroused when the Strozzi courier brought out a letter on 24 April and he noticed it was addressed to him in Lucrezia's hand; but on unfolding the paper he found it was only another letter from Ercole. Still she must have known full well it sang her praises, and Pietro wrote back chiding Ercole for letting him know nothing of the circumstances of this little caprice, not even what mood she had been in. The two friends' cult of Lucrezia fills the letters they exchanged in both Latin and Italian that spring and early summer. Like the good Petrarchan he always affected to be, Bembo confided to Ercole (which was as good as confiding in Lucrezia) that the thought of her, and of his friend's proximity to her, dulled all the delights of the country: the villa, the green meadows, the companionship of the Muses and of the great writers of the past were fast losing their appeal. It would not be long before he was writing such things to her directly.

IN the Ambrosiana Library in Milan are a few papers carefully preserved by Bembo during his long life, and all are mementos of his friendship with Lucrezia. Among them are the nine letters from her that can be read in this volume, the sole record we have of how she wrote to him, in spite of evidence that there were many others. Written between 1503 and the very last years of her short life, most are little more than brief communications but collectively they are probably more revealing than anything else that remains of her generally very non-committal correspondence. One would be hard put to find, for instance, a more terse yet intense billet-doux than Lucrezia's little note of 24 June 1503. Today what Bembo may have considered almost as great a trophy is displayed in the Ambrosiana in a kind of gold and crystal monstrance, though he himself kept it inside a folded sheet of vellum secured with ribbon: a long lock of fair hair, which no one has ever seriously doubted he obtained from Lucrezia. Some idea of how much this prize may have been coveted can be gained from the first of Bembo's sonnets included in this volume, *Di que' bei crin, che tanto più sempre amo*, generally assumed to have been written for Lucrezia. That curling tress of blond hair now exhibited like a holy relic is not entirely complete. In 1816 Byron visited the Ambrosiana and was shown Lucrezia's letters and found them 'the prettiest love letters in the world'; he committed some of them to memory since he was not allowed to make copies, and when the librarian was out of the room stole one long strand from that lock of hair, 'the prettiest and fairest imaginable'.

On the earliest Lucretian papers Bembo's small neat hand has noted the date, and the first dated sheet is a stanza of a Spanish love poem by the fifteenth century Aragonese poet Lope de Eſtúñiga. It opens our collection. In Ferrara, on 25 May 1503, Lucrezia took a big sheet of paper and copied out in her large spiky hand: *Yo pienso si me muriese* ... A little card which Bembo pasted on the back carefully records the day and place under the legend LVCRETIAE BORGIAE MANVS. This reverent inscription and Eſtúñiga's words about the torment and the glory of a great love, *tan grande amor*, suggest that Bembo may have believed that this document he preserved for the forty-three remaining years of his life already gave some indication of her feelings.

Even if his first letter to her (I) shows that for his taste such Spanish coplas were only charming trifles next to what the 'Tuscan' lyric could achieve, the words clearly acted on his fancy. Both Lucrezia and Ercole urged him to write, and within a few days he was back in Oſtellato, his head full of the 'Duchessa' and poetry. In that first gallant letter he promises further work to come and meanwhile sends a manuscript of the first book of *Gli Asolani*, with two recent sonnets, too imperfect as yet to be seen by other (more critical?) eyes, and also a 'little song' which dares to compete with her Eſtúñiga. He wrote for her in Latin, in Italian, and even in Spanish. The Ambrosiana manuscripts show how some not very impressive lines emerged only after a good deal of struggle and juggle with snatches of Spanish love poetry which she and her circle must have shown him.

Tan bivo es mi padesçer	*My grief is so alive*
Y tan muerto mi sperar;	*My hope as dead as stone*
Que ni lo un puede prender,	*For one can not revive,*
Ni lo otro quiere dexar.	*One leaves me not alone*

There is nothing to indicate which two sonnets he may have enclosed with this letter, so I have chosen to accompany it with the sonnet presumed to have been inspired by the blond hair which was Lucrezia's great pride. It reached to her waist but often she wore it plaited and held in a little silken net trimmed with jewels, such as is shown on a celebrated medallion portrait cast during her early years in Ferrara. Very probably the gold medallion which she refers to so excitedly in her first letter (II) which she had rushed out to Ostellato five days later carried some similar profile portrait, showing on its reverse the relief of a flame for which the smitten scholar-poet at once suggested the cryptically ungrammatical motto EST ANIMUM (III). The device of the flame had itself been suggested by Bembo and one wonders whether it had not become linked in their minds, or at least in his, with the fire in the copla she had copied out for him, *el fuego donde peno.* Her letter about the medallion was written not in Italian but in Spanish, for reasons of semi-secrecy perhaps, or to acknowledge his own efforts in her native tongue and mark an increasing intimacy.

No surer way of fanning the flames of that particular fire than with another visit to Ferrara. Don Alfonso was out of the country, absent on one of his frequent tours of foreign cities and fortifications which were to stand him in such good stead in the wars to come, and doubtless this facilitated closer contacts between Messer Pietro and 'la Duchessa'. Bembo spent several days in the city and seems to have gone back to Ostellato with the near certainty that to some degree she returned his feelings, although plainly he was anxious for some unequivocal assurance from her. The few lines (IV) which he wrote on his return, and the accompanying sonnet, are in their different ways fine examples of his art. 'Look in thy heart and write': the injunction is never as simple as it sounds, but at this crucial time it served Bembo well and he produced one of the most flawless sonnets he ever wrote. These lines, *Poi ch'ogni ardir mi circonscrisse Amore*, also contain the first indication of the need for dissimulation and discretion in their contacts. But how would she answer this cry from the 'crystal' of his heart?

For five days she kept him guessing. Then, on 24 June, her intense little note (V) was brought out to him. In answer to his delicate query about what she saw when she gazed into her own crystal she boldly avowed that she found what he saw in his; her letter testifies that their twin hearts have an unparalleled affinity, and may it be a gospel everlasting: *e resti per evangelio perpetuo*. Since this far overstepped the bounds of conventional courtly compliments she did not sign her name, but instructed him to write to her from now on as '*f.f.*' Bembo must have realised why these initials were particularly apt, but no single satisfactory explanation has been found. They might indicate fidelity or felicity, or simply the fire of love, *fuoco* and *fiamma* with which Bembo's effusions abound. Some have pointed out that 'f' or 'ff' was used on Vatican documents to record the papal 'fiat', recalling that Lucrezia herself had handled the Pope's correspondence on one famous occasion during her father's absence from Rome. Or it would be amusing to think that '*f.f.*' represents nothing more than the Italians' familiar abbreviation for indicating that the signatory is acting in place of another (*facente funzione*), which was exactly Lucrezia's pretence, but it does not seem to have been in use in her time. '*ff*' figures prominently in an obscure inscription (reproduced on the first page of this book) which appears on the best known of the medals cast for Lucrezia, the so-called *Amore bendato*, in which Cupid is shown disarmed and blindfolded and tied to a laurel tree, though the medal is no earlier than 1505. Is the inscription the unknown medallist's cryptic signature, or a concealed motto? The *f.f.* disguise may have been necessary to confuse the 'enemy' (although this and other *f.f.* letters are clearly in Lucrezia's hand) but it is just as likely – Lucrezia was not a Borgia for nothing – that an air of stealth and intrigue brought extra excitement, alluding at one and the same time to the temptation and the impossibility of a forbidden intimacy.

Naturally there were fellow-conspirators: Angela Borgia, and Nicola and Lisabetta, Messer Pietro's favourite girls in Lucrezia's entourage, and of course Messer Ercole was in the know. Sometimes, either when he assumed she was too closely watched or simply for the pleasure of the game, Bembo would use Lucrezia's confidantes as a screen for her (XXIII, XXX). The pretence is especially enjoyable when Bembo writes directly to Lucrezia and the thinnest fiction is that he only wants her to lend a sympathetic ear to a recital of his feelings for *f.f.* (XVI), or else when Lucrezia writes apologising a little too warmly for the silence of the phantomatic *f.f.* (XXII).

As soon as he received her note of 24 June Bembo wrote back exultantly that he now felt capable of a noble and heroic love (VI). While anxiously awaiting her word he had worked on three sonnets inspired by a compensatory dream in which she had seemed to reassure him his suffering was not in vain. Three sonnets concerning such an experience (although the matter of the verse was found as much in Petrarch as in his dreams) appear in Bembo's collected *Rime* and one is included here: *Se'l viver men che pria m'è duro e vile* After his first passionate enthusiasm his next communications show a new playfulness, as if he is quite sure of her and is now all buoyant expectancy. She felt depressed by certain events in Ferrara and needed to see him, but owing to a strained neck he had to put off his coming until the start of July (VII, VIII).

At this point a gap in the frequency of the correspondence indicates that Bembo spent a gratifying fortnight and more in Ferrara, of which a glimpse is afforded by his teasing note of 14 July (IX). The cult of Lucrezia, whose simple gospel had been spelled out to him in her poignant note three weeks earlier, was proving to be the true faith indeed, and all the better if a little tantalising. We know from many reports that at this time his idol used to dress in dark Florentine and Venetian velvets to set off the smouldering Borgia rubies and the many ropes of pearls, and that long golden hair of hers. On the 14th he felt some detail of her head-dress was worn secretly for him, a heart-shaped pendant perhaps, or a single diamond, or the large emerald cut flat and hanging from a jewelled ferronière above her brow, which Laura Bentivoglio once described enviously to another Duchess. From this letter and the one that follows (X) one feels that Bembo no longer made much effort to conceal his adulation, even from those well outside the conspiracy. Perhaps she was especially reckless and irresistible in those weeks, newly in love, and basking in the reflected glory of her brother Cesare whose spreading conquests and ruthless exploits and seemingly endless good fortune were the talk and the terror of Italy. 'Such a gospel and so many miracles . . .' Petrarch reborn had found his Laura, and what is more she was a real princess.

The days were sweet, and parting, even if it meant going no further than Ostellato, was a bitter-sweet pang. Messer Pietro's tender letters of farewell to *f.f.* (X, XI), though he promises to be back so soon, seem to say the long road stretches away for a thousand miles. She had seemed unwell on the day he left, and a week later she wrote to him saying she had recovered from two bouts of fever. Among the slow-running rivers and canals of Ferrara, the long dykes and marshes, few ever escaped the effects of malaria. As summer wore on plague also came to the city, as it did almost every year with varying intensity, and the first deaths were reported. In the same days a virulent epidemic of *malaria perniciosa* was spreading through Rome. On 3 August Bembo wrote impatiently to Strozzi wondering if he was ever coming out to animate the quiet of Ostellato. Finally his restlessness got the better of him and he went back into the city; and now it was his turn to fall ill, and hers to comfort him. On 11 August, presumably chaperoned by some of her girls, Lucrezia left the Castelvecchio to call at Bembo's house, and stay at his bedside 'a long while'. The next morning all Messer Pietro's fever had vanished and he was well enough to write (XIII) and acknowledge the miraculous cure her celestial presence had effected, almost as if she had fulfilled the vision described in the dream-sonnets. He went back to Ostellato to convalesce, and Lucrezia also left the insalubrious city to take up residence at Medelana, an Este summer villa which lay conveniently close to Ostellato.

But within a week she received shattering news. Unknown to her, on 12 August, the very day Bembo had written to report the effect of her angelic medicine, her father and brother had both fallen desperately ill in Rome with the fever, though naturally rumours held they had been poisoned. Cesare was still only in his twenties and after six days his condition very slightly improved; but for the 72-year-old Pontiff, vigorous though his constitution certainly was (his last child had been born earlier that year), no angels saw fit to devise a cure. On the contrary, as Francesco Gonzaga wrote to his wife Isabella d'Este, witnesses attested that seven devils were seen round his bed at the moment he expired, which proved that he had secured the Papacy by a pact with Satan. Alexander VI died on the afternoon of 18 August, after a reign of twelve zestful and eventful years, and on the third anniversary of the murder of Alfonso Bisceglie. The news reached Medelana the following day.

On the 21st Bembo arrived from Ostellato to express his sympathy and was disturbed by the transformation he saw. She was inconsolable in her despair and hardly seemed to acknowledge him. In the famous letter of condolence to her Ladyship (XIV) there is little hint of *f.f.* until the end, but beneath the measured eloquence of the dutiful courtier and sage counsellor one may detect resentment that her grief for her 'very great father' could so estrange them. She should care more for the living than the dead, and also look to her own welfare at such a dangerous time. Everyone knew that with the Pope buried and Cesare Borgia seemingly too unwell to maintain control either in Rome or Romagna the precarious little Borgia empire would sooner or later collapse, and if she herself hoped to survive the fall she would need to show some of her well-tried stamina, even be grateful she had married an Este. Messer Pietro claimed to shed tears of sympathy but not many other eyes were moist in Ferrara. The Borgia alliances had never been sentimental, valued no more than the power they endorsed or the fears they purported to allay. Her father-in-law even declined to order the court into mourning and privately expressed his satisfaction that Providence had seen fit to remove such a 'great scandal' from the Church. Louis XII, once a powerful advocate of the Este-Borgia union, voiced Lucrezia's greatest fear when he asked the Ferrarese envoy what purpose he supposed was served by her marriage now.

Nevertheless, as in the case of her previous 'adversities', soon Lucrezia rallied, particularly when she received news that her brother was on his feet again and apparently still had the upper hand in Rome. She set about raising money for Cesare and tried to persuade Ercole d'Este to supply troops for the security of Romagna, and in fact he did offer 200 men when he recognised that Cesare was still a force to be reckoned with. But all hinged on Alexander's successor, since Cesare's credibility depended on his being reconfirmed Vicar-General of the papal army. Towards the end of September the frail and elderly Cardinal Piccolomini was elected Pius III; he was not known to be an outspoken enemy of the Borgias but his election promised only a little respite since his days were clearly numbered. As Lucrezia's tension and anxieties eased a little it was only natural that she should seek again the reassurance and sentimental distraction of Bembo's 'steadfast diamond'. On 4 October, when Messer Pietro heard her reaffirm that he enjoyed her favour, he resented only that she had not trusted their 'affinity' enough to allay his fears a little earlier. Part of the memorable letter which he went home to write in a blaze of love (XV) betrays the difficulties they experienced in reaching a new understanding. But now he has his *f.f.* again, and once more dreams of accomplishing great deeds for her. All else is a thing of the past, let her burn all his letters and keep just this one as pledge of an undying love.

There followed five intense days in which it seems he spent many pleasant hours in Medelana, including one memorable moment when she spoke to him alone 'on the balcony with the moon as witness' (XVI). Then, with little warning, on 10 October he left for Venice; and when he had to go she appeared ill with anxiety: 'of your being indisposed on the day I took my leave I shall say no more.' But why such a sudden departure?

Three days earlier, on 7 October, Don Alfonso and his court had arrived at the Strozzi villa in Ostellato for some hunting. Perhaps, as Maria Bellonci suggests in her fine biography of Lucrezia, Don Alfonso's informants had reported 'too many kisses' and her husband's descent on Ostellato was an act of intimidation. Even if Bembo's departure for Venice was in answer to an urgent summons and not an excuse to escape some real or imagined threat it is still possible that his father and brother were anxious to extricate him from what they must by now have realised was a hopeless and even dangerous infatuation. In the earliest days of his absence he composed and sent to her a sonnet, *L'alta cagion, che da principio diede*, inspired by another copla she had shown him, and in it he figures as the heliotrope that must see her sun. From 'Noniano', as the family called their riverside villa at Santa Maria di Non a few miles from Padua, he wrote to *f.f.* to say he had been delayed due to an accident to his father but after attending to other business would be back in Ostellato to see again his 'own dear half' (XVII). However on 2 November, once more in Ferrara, he reports he is prevented from going out to Ostellato (XVIII). The only serious excuse he offers – that he has been told there are no provisions for him in the villa owing to Don Alfonso's visit – is so odd that it is tempting to believe that Alfonso really had had more than he was prepared to tolerate of this amorous Venetian. While the plague continued in Ferrara Lucrezia remained in Medelana and Pietro waited 'respectfully'. Other records show that there was talk of her visiting the Pio family at Carpi, in which case Bembo might have gone there to meet her, but sickness among her household compelled her to abandon the project. But by now Lucrezia had far greater worries. Pope Pius was dead and Giuliano della Rovere, the Borgias' most determined adversary, had swiftly been elected Pope Julius II. In late November news reached her that Cesare was Julius's prisoner in Rome. From this moment until four years later when she heard of Cesare's death in a skirmish in the Pyrenees after eluding the Pope's surveillance and then again escaping from a fortress in Spain, Lucrezia worked tirelessly and quite uselessly to persuade her powerful contacts to do something for her brother. Meantime his two children, Girolamo and Camilla Lucrezia, were taken into her care.

She did not return to the city from Medelana until late December. Bembo had promised to spend the entire winter in Ferrara, yet she was hardly reinstalled in the Castle when he was once again called away to Venice. He arranged a last meeting during which, seemingly affected by a sense of foreboding, each opened the pages of a Bible at random to divine what lay in store. Bembo's eyes lighted on a verse about the death of Solomon, which must have deeply disturbed his superstitious mind. On reaching Venice he was told that Carlo Bembo had died on 30 December and was already buried (XIX). 'Oh, accursed and barbarous evil destiny!' he laments in his first letter to her, and indeed the death of his devoted younger brother was not only a personal tragedy but also had implications for his future. To judge by what he says, valuable support from Carlo had given him a measure of freedom to think and write and lead the agreeable life of a man of letters. Old Bernardo Bembo was seventy now, and still burdened with duties. The truth that Messer Pietro would not be returning to Ferrara for a very long while must have struck Madonna Lucrezia with especial force when she read that he had sent to Ferrara for all his books.

Though few letters have survived, they wrote fitfully to each other over the next months, the 'faithful heliotrope' being the better correspondent. For practical reasons communications could not be as frequent now since they had to rely on trusted servants or mutual friends who happened to be journeying between Ferrara and Venice. As always, Messer Ercole was glad to oblige. In late March her Majordomo brought news that she looked lovelier than ever and planned to come to Venice at Ascensiontide (XXI). With high hopes he wrote to her, but we find her on the very next day (29 March) writing to him from Ferrara in answer to an earlier depressed letter, and with no mention of a visit to Venice. Perhaps when her letter was conveyed to him the bearer told him not to expect her after all, and certainly his reply (XXIII) is again despondent, even desperate. This letter, and hers of 29 March, so strictly apply the *f.f.* subterfuge that one senses not only that the need for secrecy is now more real than ever before but that the invented creature truly does mask a third presence, the common memory that neither must allow to dim despite the difficulties of separation. During that troubled spring Bembo presented himself as candidate for Venetian embassies to France, Germany and Spain, but in each case was outvoted in the

Senate by large majorities. Exhausted and depressed he took to his bed in May (XXIV), and *f.f.* broke silence to communicate her concern (XXV).

Messages, but it seems no further letters, reached Pietro through intermediaries during the following months. He eventually pulled himself together, though the tragic note persists, and also the feeling that the good days are irrecoverable. Messer Ercole sometimes brought news of her, but time and again he postponed his promised visit to Ferrara, very likely because it would not have been wise to return. August and September were spent in the family villa at Santa Maria di Non where, he assured her, he intended to write 'pages about you that will be read a century after we are gone' (XXVI). She had experienced enough 'dark things and horrors and tears' in recent times, but just what Bembo refers to in this letter is not clear, perhaps simply the description given to him by the courtier and poet Ercole Pio who had recently passed through Ferrara, though from Bembo's letter XXXI one gathers she experienced another fruitless pregnancy during this year. Nothing came of Bembo's resolve to write memorable things of her, apart from the long and rather formal dedicatory letter at the front of *Gli Asolani*. Perhaps the gift of that book may be seen as a substitute for the great work for her which he was certainly in no condition to write. How anxious she was to see *Gli Asolani* in print is clear from Pietro's next letter (XXVII), and yet the author seems suddenly plunged in gloom about its prospects. Travelling the country in October he thinks of visiting her, but in Verona hears rumours that Duke Ercole lies dying, and concludes that this is no time to show his face in Ferrara (XXVIII). Again, writing in November, he insists that he has been constantly on the point of coming (XXIX). But there are no more letters that year, Christmas comes and goes and Messer Pietro is still in Venice. On 25 January 1505, as he is soon to learn, Ercole d'Este finally breathed his last. Alfonso will duly have succeeded to the ducal throne, and

Lucrezia will be reigning Duchess. The long-awaited book on which he had staked his reputation was now with the printer and it could bear a splendid address: *A Madonna Lucrezia Borgia Estense Duchessa Illustrissima di Ferrara.*

Nothing is known of the circumstances of Bembo's reappearance in Ferrara in early February 1505, but it seems possible that he accompanied informally some Venetian mission to congratulate the new Duke and Duchess. At such a time it is extraordinary that she managed to slip him a letter containing what he describes as the most gratifying avowal of love that he ever received, and which in turn prompted the most desperate and explicit and longest letter he ever penned to her (XXX). The letter's unusual length may be due to the likelihood that they had had little or no time together unobserved, but more evidently to the fact that it is a valiant refusal to accept the inevitable, a brave attempt to persuade her to keep their love alive for all the long years ahead during which 'Fortune' is not likely to alter for the better. Nowhere else are the risks involved in their friendship so forthrightly expressed: 'Do not trust anyone, no matter whom . . . Take good care not to be seen writing . . . If I am still alive . . .' This time he wrote under cover of a letter to *Madonna N.,* almost certainly Nicola, the Duchessa's lively Sienese lady-in-waiting, recently married to a member of the powerful Trotti family of Ferrara (Nicola had written to console Bembo during the bad days following the death of his brother, and in his reply he had spoken of their closeness as of that between brother and sister). The letter tells of conditions in which it has been impossible to communicate with her (in fact four months had passed without a letter recorded between them, though one from him apparently reached her shortly before his arrival), a situation in which their love is obstructed by 'a thousand separations, a thousand watchmen, a thousand barriers, and a thousand walls'. But the immediate arrangements are clear enough, she can get a long letter to him via the unnamed bearer (Ercole Pio?)

who is able to penetrate the guard around her and will call upon her on his return from Carpi; and Messer Pietro himself, as promised at their meeting, will be back in Ferrara 'after Easter', and thence on to Rome. On many other occasions he had made elegant play of the hand-kiss that was ordinarily the most conventional conclusion to a letter, but because of the warm yet chaste tone of their correspondence there is little to lead one to anticipate the sensuality of the imagined kiss on 'one of those prettiest and brightest and sweetest eyes' and the erotic thoughts that accompany the gift of the little keepsake Agnus Dei which may touch where he may not, a last forceful yet wistful admission that the only possible form of intimacy between them is epistolary.

As promised, Bembo did return to Ferrara after Easter. For a year and a half Bernardo Bembo had been standing by to head an important Venetian mission to Rome to congratulate Julius II on his election, but because of the fiery Pope's wrath over the Republic's seizure of part of Romagna after Cesare Borgia's demise, the journey had continually been deferred. Now the party, the old senator's last foreign mission, was preparing to leave, and his son, with hopes of using his own and his father's good contacts to make a career in Rome, was to accompany the delegation. He left a day or two ahead of the others in order to pass through Ferrara and join up with the company during the passage south. Since the Aldine press had just published *Gli Asolani* the previous month it seems likely that Bembo brought a presentation copy with him so that he could personally offer the Duchess the book he had dedicated to her. But no more is known than that Bembo was reported in Ferrara on 9 April 1505, and that he passed through the city again two months later on his return from Rome; by which time Lucrezia must have been very visibly carrying the child that was born in September. In the years to come Lucrezia and Pietro wrote from time to time, but there is no evidence that they ever saw each other again.

THAT concludes the phase of greatest interest, thirty known letters exchanged in the twenty months between June 1503 and February 1505, and thereafter the correspondence, like the passion, quickly lost urgency. What follows is little more than an extended epilogue, with letters ranging in date from later in 1505 until the last years of Lucrezia's life. Our edition of the letters is divided into two parts to reflect these two phases. Although nothing that survives of the first phase has been excluded from Part One, Part Two is not quite so comprehensive. The reader will find all five of the remaining letters by Lucrezia, but of the thirteen Bembo letters which survive eight have seemed sufficient to give the flavour of these later more formal exchanges. Part Two opens with three letters from Bembo dating still from 1505 but which already convey the altered nature of the communications between them; a more dutiful and public address by Messer Pietro, her 'meanest servant', sometimes alleviated by small hints of their former intimacy, though nothing as precise as the nostalgic reference to 'good Messer Ercole's Ostellato' in letter XXXII will occur again. From these first letters one may also infer Bembo's continuing dissatisfaction with his life (Rome had been exhilarating but had yielded nothing concrete in the way of lucrative or congenial employment) and therefore a still quite urgent need to remind the Duchess of his existence. All three letters concern the birth of the son she so much needed in order to confirm her status in Ferrara; but sadly this baby, Alessandro, survived only twenty-five days, and it was to be another three years, and at least one more miscarriage, before Duke Alfonso received a strong young heir.

In the years between 1506 and 1513, at least on the evidence of what remains, Lucrezia and Bembo felt little need to communicate, though this near silence could be attributed to the fact that during much of this time Ferrara and Urbino, where Bembo settled, were on opposite sides in war. The period only numbers three extant letters, each from Bembo, none being reproduced here: a hasty note from Urbino in 1506, and two extremely formal epistles of congratulation on the births of children, Ercole in 1508 and Ippolito in 1509. Both sons survived, Ercole eventually to succeed his father as Duke in 1534, and Ippolito to become the Cardinal for whom the Villa d'Este at Tivoli was created.

During these years Ferrara was almost permanently at war, first in the League of Cambrai allied with Pope Julius II against Venice when Alfonso d'Este was Captain General of the armies of the Church, and then against Julius when the bellicose Pope reversed his policies allying himself with the Venetians, Ferrara's old enemies, to drive her one powerful ally, France, out of Italy. During the long emergency Lucrezia's jewellery and plate were pawned, Ferrarese territory shrank, and the beleaguered town was only saved from certain capture by the timely death of the Pope in 1513. In these grim years, Alfonso, excommunicated and declared dispossessed, came into his own as a great commander, & at the battle of Ravenna in 1512 the French and Ferrarese checked the combined forces of the Pope and Venice and Spain, largely due to the murderous effect of Alfonso's artillery. In his absences Lucrezia acted as co-regent with Cardinal Ippolito and also contributed significantly to the vital alliance with France by playing the great hostess, entertaining French officers with a style that deeply impressed these connoisseurs of latter-day chivalry. Among them were such celebrated figures as Gaston de Foix and the Chevalier Bayard, whose faithful biographer called the Duchess of Ferrara 'la plus triompante princesse', a veritable pearl of this world, beautiful, kind, gentle and chivalrous to all when she presided in her Castle over splendid banquets and parties 'à la mode d'Italie'. On a more personal level, apart from her children's births, three tragic losses marked these years. She received the shock of Cesare's death in 1507, to be followed in 1508 by the assassination of Ercole Strozzi, her most loyal friend in Ferrara. He was found one summer morning in a street in the inner city, wrapped in his cloak with his crutches beside him, and with twenty-two dagger-thrusts in his body. In the middle of the night, riding home from a dinner-party, he had been dragged from his mule and murdered. Messer Ercole had been leading a perilous life directing a secret intrigue between Lucrezia and her brother-in-law Francesco Gonzaga, the Marquis of Mantua. The Duchess had won the admiration of Isabella d'Este's husband as early as 1504, shortly after the departure of Bembo, when she had used all her charm to persuade this soldier-hero who had withstood the French at Fornovo during her father's reign to use his influence to further her brother's hopeless cause in Italy. Communications between them had intensified when her hopes were raised by news of Cesare's escape from prison in Spain, and on her behalf her devoted Messer Ercole penned some of the love-letters which he and his brother Guido conveyed to the Marquis under code names. Though he risked antagonising both Isabella and Alfonso (unless the latter had political reasons for abetting the intrigue) the most likely explanation for Ercole's assassination is presumed to be his recent marriage to the fascinating Barbara Torelli, a talented poetess and widow of a brutal Bentivoglio who had once been a captain in Cesare Borgia's army, for the Bentivogli resented a man not of their choice marrying the heiress to a considerable fortune. Lucrezia received further sad news in 1512 when she heard that her first child, Rodrigo Bisceglie, whose welfare had always deeply concerned her, had died amid his little court in Puglia. Increasingly she took to spending periods of retreat from the strain of public life in her favourite convent of Corpus Domini. In 1510, or earlier, she founded her own convent of San Bernardino in the palace of the Romei family, beneath whose walls Messer Ercole's blood-soaked body had been found.

Other matters, and other flirtations, now held Messer Pietro's attention. Six agreeable and creative years were spent in the Duchy of Urbino where he was one of the most popular and cultured ornaments of that brilliant little court whose social ideals and intellectual concerns were immortalised by his close friend Count Baldessar Castiglione in *The Book of the Courtier*. It may even be true to say that the once-renowned author of *Gli Asolani* is better known today as a character in another's book: that gallant and learned Pietro Bembo who in *The Courtier* defends the superiority of letters over arms and provides the climax to the work with his impassioned discourse on the noble love appropriate to the courtier who is no longer young. Anyone who knows that amiable masterpiece, which did so much to form the European ideal of the courtier and gentleman, will already be familiar with several of the names encountered in the correspondence between Bembo and Lucrezia. Ercole Pio (XXVI) was the brother of Emilia Pio who in *The Courtier* along with her friend the Duchess of Urbino represents the perfect gentlewoman; Alfonso Ariosto (XXVII, XXVIII), 'a most civil and judicious young gentleman' whom Bembo had recommended for Lucrezia's service, developed into the perfect courtier to whom Castiglione first dedicated his book; Bernardo Dovizi da Bibbiena (XXXV, XXXVI), in the book given a long disquisition on the kinds of joke that courtiers may crack in polite company, was one of the most lionised wits and successful playwrights of his age and Bembo's closest friend after the death of Ercole Strozzi. As personal secretary to Cardinal Giuliano de' Medici, Bibbiena provides the link between Bembo's Urbino years and his later career in Rome; for when in March 1513 his master was elected Pope Leo X Bibbiena's powers of persuasion helped to secure for his friend the post of Papal Secretary. For several years Bembo shared this distinguished office with another celebrated Latinist, Jacopo Sadoleto, an old friend from Ferrara days, and their principal duty was to draft the papal breves in which they set a standard of Ciceronian Latin that was for a time an accepted model for official and learned communications both in Italy and abroad.

The nature of his Vatican duties made Bembo uniquely well informed about papal policies and his old connections with Ferrara could now prove very useful in the Duchy's attempts to resume good relations after a long war with the Church. At first the new Pope was assumed to be a friend to Ferrara but soon a hostile policy began to emerge, which made it all the more important for the Este, including Lucrezia, to cultivate potential allies at the heart of the Vatican. No man at that cultivated and extravagant court was more vital to reach than Bembo's great friend, Bibbiena, whose influence upon the luxury-loving Leo was soon so evident that he earned the nickname of 'the other Pope', *alter papa*. Lucrezia already knew Bibbiena well and she made full use of the connection in diplomatic exchanges between Ferrara and Rome. On Leo's election Bibbiena had been made Papal Treasurer, and later that year was created Cardinal. His swift career to the top encouraged Bembo's own hopes of a cardinalate but the failure of a delicate mission to Venice probably put paid to his chances. Nine or ten years earlier, with no employment, he had repeatedly written to Lucrezia begging her to make use of his services, and still, she discovered, he was ready to oblige. She may have felt his new position to be an agreeable confirmation of her earlier high estimation of him, but the fact that the sudden renewal of their correspondence dates from Bembo's elevation to a position of considerable influence in Rome is evidence enough that her motives were not purely nostalgic.

Duke Alfonso was himself in Rome in April 1513 to congratulate the new Pope and to have the removal of Julius II's censures against him formally endorsed, and his courtiers made a special point of conveying 'many affectionate greetings' to the new Papal Secretary from the distant Duchess (XXXIV). The second letter (XXXV) which Bembo wrote to her after his appointment betrays a scarcely repressed delight in his new eminence and also nicely illustrates the mood of friendly rivalry between himself and the 'Monsignor

Treasurer'. Through Bembo's good offices Lucrezia wished to secure a breve of absolution confirming the indulgences she had enjoyed under Alexander VI and Julius II. The letter 'entirely in your own hand' which Bembo jokingly made a condition of the granting of absolution duly arrived (XXXVI), and it is a very successful attempt to rival the wit of Bembo's 'very beautiful letter'. Indeed, if it is all her own work, it is a precious little record of Lucrezia's savoir-faire.

Her next letter (XXXVII) again shows how she made use of Bembo to expedite her interests. If the year of the letter really is 1514 then her poor state of health was probably due to the imminent arrival of a third son, Alessandro, born in early April, only to die at the age of two. Sometimes Bembo's services received tangible reward, including on one occasion 'a beautiful little cap' referred to in a letter (XXXVIII) which he gave to the Papal Nuncio, Latino Juvenale, who was leaving the same day for Ferrara to represent the Pope at her little Ercole's confirmation. The conclusion to this letter already suggests Bembo's sense of frustration in a post which was proving to be so demanding that it left him little time for other writing, and in fact as his health suffered and his chances of advancement receded he came more and more to resent the 'slavery' of his official commitments. By this time relations between the new Pope and Ferrara were very strained, and this explains Lucrezia's special plea to Bembo to assure Leo as often as possible of her 'most devoted service' (XXXIX). Neither during his Venetian mission in December 1514 nor on subsequent occasions when papal business took him within easy reach of Ferrara did Bembo find time to visit the city and 'pay his respects' to her Ladyship. In a gallant letter of 1515 (XLI) which his literary protégé and secretary Agostino Beazzano carried to the Duchess from neighbouring Bologna in answer to four warm lines from her (XL) he promises to come 'after Carnival' without fail; and again when writing in haste from Bologna two years later he expresses the hope of being able to see her 'at some less busy time' (XLII). Pious hopes only, one cannot help feeling.

The letter (XLIII) which I have placed last in this collection may very well belong a little earlier but since it cannot be assigned to any precise date I have used it as a poignant little end-piece to conclude this fifteen or sixteen-year correspondence. Lucrezia, in spite of the success she made of her role as Duchess of Ferrara, must often have had need of that cure for despair which, as she reminds Bembo, he once passed on to her. Apart from her considerable responsibilities during very perilous years for the Duchy, she received news of the death of her brother Jofrè in 1517, of her mother in 1518, and then of the Marquis of Mantua, her last flame, who succumbed to the effects of syphilis in early 1519. It seems Lucrezia was not well enough to attend the state funeral in Mantua at which the Pope's representative, it so happens, was Pietro Bembo. There were also the anxieties of her many pregnancies. Despite Lucrezia's romantic yearnings Alfonso had always asserted his indisputable possession of her body, never sparing her the rigours of child-bearing except when war kept him from Ferrara. If I have counted right, during seventeen years she bore him nine children, of whom four sons and one daughter survived, the others being still-born or dying in their infancy; and this is to leave out of account several miscarriages, one of which, it was her infuriated husband's complaint, had been caused by her dancing too exuberantly with the Marquis of Mantua. During Lucrezia's first summer in Ferrara a difficult pregnancy had nearly killed her, and the summer of 1519 found her desperately ill for the same reason. She gave birth on 14 June to a still-born daughter, and in the grip of puerperal fever, feeling that she would not recover, wrote to Rome for the Pope's benediction. Lucrezia Borgia died on the night of 24 June 1519, at the age of thirty-nine. Contemporary eulogies described her as a conscientious administrator, fair in hearing the petitions of citizens, a very affectionate mother, a devout Christian justly celebrated for her good works and for the charities she founded, and reputed during the later years to have worn a hairshirt beneath her court dresses. Alfonso d'Este seemed genuinely affected by her death but not long afterwards instated Laura Dianti, the buxom daughter of a local hat-maker, as his official companion.

As for Pietro Bembo, he was fifty before he finally managed to extricate himself completely from papal service after a period of repeated ill-health and exhaustion. In 1522 he settled down happily to a new life in Padua with a young woman of humble origin, almost certainly an ex-courtesan, named Morosina, whom he had first known in Rome. In spite of his taking the vows of the order of St John of Jerusalem, Morosina was to bear him three children, and his letters show convincingly that he loved her and his little family tenderly. By now he was an immensely celebrated and revered figure, dignified by a flowing white beard. He divided his time between his house in Padua and the Villa Bozza in glorious retirement amid the affection of his family and friends and the admiration of his disciples, working at his papers, keeping up a vast international correspondence, and adding to his great collection of rare manuscripts, antique and modern marbles and bronzes, gems and coins and contemporary paintings. In 1525 he brought out his *Prose della volgar lingua*, an authoritative treatise on the literary language; in 1530 appeared a revised edition of *Gli Asolani* and also his collected *Rime*, which saw at least forty editions before the end of the century; there followed the reissue of various Latin works and publication of the breves he had composed for Pope Leo X; as the official historiographer of Venice he wrote a contemporary *Historia Veneta* in both Latin and Italian. His fondest worldly hopes were realised finally in 1539 when he received his Cardinal's hat, being celebrated in the nomination as 'indisputably foremost in learning and eloquence in this our age', though even such ecclesiastical eminence did not hinder him writing an occasional sonnet to celebrate his last infatuation, for the young Elisabetta Querini. The Most Reverend Monsignor Pietro Bembo,

Cardinal of San Clemente, Bishop of Bergamo, Knight of Rhodes, Prior of Hungary, died on 18 January 1547 in Rome, aged seventy-six.

IN view of their intrinsic interest and their authors' renown, it is curious that the letters between Lucrezia Borgia and Pietro Bembo have never been brought together in a single volume, and never before extensively translated. Lucrezia's nine letters (ms. H.246 in the Ambrosiana, numbers II and XXV written in Spanish) were published long ago by Bernardo Gatti, *Lettere di Lucrezia Borgia a Messer Pietro Bembo*, Milan, 1859. Bembo's side of the correspondence has had to be assembled from various sources published and unpublished. Letters to the unidentified *f.f.* and, in a separate section, to Lucrezia, first appeared in the last of four volumes of Bembo's Italian correspondence published in Venice in 1552 by Gualtiero Scotto. This Venetian Walter Scott, like his namesake, knew where to draw the line, and alerted his discreet readers to the fact that he had deleted 'certain things which it would not be good for everyone to know'. However, diplomacy rather than prudery seems to have determined most deletions, and all the evidence points to the fact that Cardinal Bembo himself had a hand in this censorship before his death. In order to come closer to the actual text of the letters he sent to Lucrezia I have used ms. Ital. 1005 in the Bibliothèque Nationale, Paris, a more reliable reflection of the lost originals since it can be used to correct obvious errors of transcription and dating and supplies the matter of a number of significant excisions from Scotto's edition, including the total omission of several letters. This manuscript is itself not complete but wherever possible I have used it for the texts and dates adopted. For all other letters my authority has been Bembo's *Opere in volgare* (Florence, 1961) edited by Mario Marti, which includes a 'Giunta' of several letters not found in Scotto's collection. I have followed the usual distinctions between letters to *f.f.* and letters to Lucrezia, except for XVI which is surely addressed to Lucrezia and not their fictitious friend, although here the subterfuge is particularly transparent. In the case of the sonnets I have applied the opposite approach and ignoring earlier less polished versions, in accordance with Bembo's belief that a poem has no object but its own perfection, have reproduced and translated from the definitive posthumous edition of the *Rime*. The epigram on Lucrezia's portrait is among the 'Lucretian' papers in the Ambrosiana, and *Yo pienso si me muriese* is transcribed from Lucrezia's autograph in the same collection. As explained, five letters from Bembo to Lucrezia, written in or after 1505, have been omitted. If the dedicatory letter to *Gli Asolani* is felt to be another omission it can be read in R. B. Gottfried's excellent English version of *Gli Asolani* (Bloomington, 1954).

Books and articles of most value in preparing this work have been:

B. MORSOLIN *Pietro Bembo e Lucrezia Borgia* (Nuova Antologia, 52, 1885)

F. GREGOROVIUS *Lucrezia Borgia* (London, 1903)

E. G. GARDNER *Dukes and Poets in Ferrara* (London, 1904)

M. CATALANO *Lucrezia Borgia, Duchessa di Ferrara* (Ferrara, 1925)

M. BELLONCI *Lucrezia Borgia; sua vita e suoi tempi* (revised edition, Milan, 1960; abridged English edition, London, 1953)

M. MALLETT *The Borgias: Rise and Fall of a Renaissance Dynasty* (London, 1969)

N. RUBINSTEIN *Lucrezia Borgia* (Rome, 1971)

C. DIONISOTTI (Editor) Bembo's *Prose e rime* (Turin, 1966), and his entry under *Pietro Bembo* in the *Dizionario biografico degli italiani*, vol 8.

C. H. CLOUGH *Pietro Bembo's 'Gli Asolani' of 1505* (Modern Language Notes, vol 84, no. 1, 1969)

Special thanks are due to David Burnett who first put me in touch with the Libanus Press, to Michael Mitchell who thought of the project and has shown such care and craftsmanship in his roles of editor and printer, to Richard Shirley Smith who has assured our work some real permanence, to Cecil Clough for expert historical advice and very valuable assistance in dating Lucrezia's letters, and to David Crane and Michael Ayton for help in figuring out the Latin of Bembo and Strozzi. A grant from the University of Durham enabled me to visit Ferrara in 1979.

All quotations in Bembo's letters are, typically, drawn from the Italian verses of Petrarch.

Dates and places of writing are enclosed in brackets if conjectural.

The Letters

PART ONE
1503 to 1505

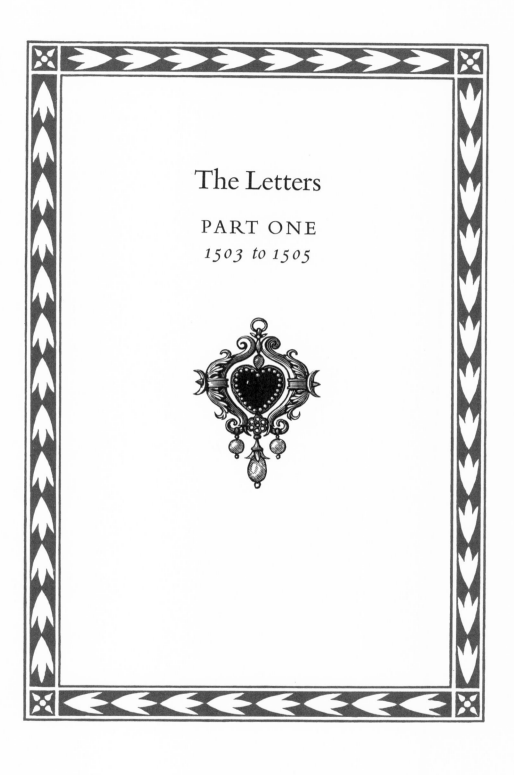

Yo pienso si me muriese
y con mis males finase
desear,
tan grande amor fenesciese
que todo el mundo quedase
sin amar.
Mas esto considerando,
mi tarde morir es luego
tanto bueno,
que devo razon usando
gloria sentir en el fuego
donde peno.

LUCRETIAE BORGIAE MANUS
Octavo Kal. Junii MDIII Ferrariae

I think were I to die
And with my wealth of pain
      Cease longing,
Such great love to deny
Could make the world remain
      Unloving.
When I consider this,
Death's long delay is all
      I must desire,
Since reason tells me bliss
Is felt by one in thrall
      To such a fire.

In the hand of Lucrezia Borgia
Ferrara 25 May 1503

*T*WO *sonnets born to me these last days, being somewhat countrified on account of their place of birth and poorly clothed, were abashed at my proposal that they should enter your Ladyship's presence; but I have given them heart by assuring them that to you they need bring nothing but fidelity, which they tell me they have in abundance. Thus emboldened they come to you, bearing a little song born this very day as rival to your own,* Yo pienso si me muriese; *and nonetheless it kneels to yours and freely concedes that the engaging tendernesses of Spanish compositions have no home in the grave purity of the Tuscan tongue, and if set therein appear neither native nor true, but false and foreign. May it please your Ladyship not to permit these lines to leave your keeping, and likewise allow none but myself to send them to you refashioned in due time, for it seldom happens to me that I leave my verses to age in the form I give them when first set down, time discovering and revealing many blemishes that the love and heat of birth veil and conceal from one. If your Ladyship will do me this favour then I shall more readily send you some other things as days go by – to which I am spurred by your most sweet commands and the love I bear my good Messer Ercole† who holds your honour dearer than his own life, and the mighty chain of obligations which your great goodness to me has fastened with a thousand links about my neck. I have no more to tell you save that this quiet retreat, these pleasant shades, this solitary life, these hideaways, which I so cherished in the past, now seem a little less pleasing to me than in former times, and content me not half so much as they were wont to do. What this may betoken, or what affliction presage, I would ask your Ladyship to seek out from her books, so that I may know whether they accord* *with mine. And now I commend myself to your kind favour as many times as there be leaves in this garden upon which I gaze, while leaning from a cool and charming little window, and write to you. Farewell.*

I am sending your Ladyship the first book of Gli Asolani *which I received this very hour.*

Ostellato   3 June 1503

† Ercole Strozzi

Di que' bei crin, che tanto più sempre amo,
Quanto maggior mio mal nasce da loro,
Sciolto era il nodo, che del bel tesoro
M'asconde quel, ch'io più di mirar bramo;
E 'l cor, che 'ndarno or, lasso, a me richiamo,
Volò subitamente in quel dolce oro,
E fe' come augellin tra verde alloro,
Ch'a suo diletto va di ramo in ramo.
Quando ecco due man belle oltra misura,
Raccogliendo le treccie al collo sparse,
Strinservi dentro lui, che v'era involto.
Gridai ben io, ma le voci fe' scarse
Il sangue, che gelò per la paura:
Intanto il cor mi fu legato e tolto.

The glowing hair I love despite my plight,
Since love abounds the more I feel the smart,
Had slipped the snood which keeps the rarest part
Of all the gold I crave locked out of sight;
When (alas, past recall now from his flight)
Into that silken hoard straight winged my heart,
As might a fledgling to green laurel dart
Then go from bough to bough in his delight.
Whereat two hands lovely beyond compare
Gathering the loosened tresses to her nape
Entangled him within, and bound them taut.
Cry as I would, the voice that did escape
Lacked any strength, my blood had chilled for fear:
Therewith the heart was torn from me and caught.

*T*RUSTING *in your skill which I appreciated these past days when considering certain designs for medallions, and having decided to have one made according to that most subtle and most apt suggestion you gave me, I thought I would send it to you with this letter, and lest it be mixed with some other element that could detract from its value I thought also to ask you herewith kindly to take the trouble for love of me to think what text should be put upon it; and for both the one matter and the other I shall remain as obliged to you as you deserve and the work must be esteemed. I await your reply with great anticipation.*

Prepared for your command
Lucretia de Borgia

Ferrara 8 June 1503

I DO confess I am in no wise able to render thanks for your great courtesy, and yet I do not repent my being so infinitely in your debt since it is enough that my heart be set on convincing you in some measure one day that my spirit is not as meagre and petty as is my lot. And if all other means to achieve this are prevented me, nothing can prevent me from ever adoring your name. As for the fire on the gold medallion which your Ladyship has sent me with the request that I should devise a motto for inscription, I can think of giving it no nobler location than the soul. Wherefore you might have it thus inscribed: *EST ANIMUM. I* did not wish to detain your courier too long, although further things might have occurred to me upon this theme, and I have undertaken the task solely to do your bidding and not because I believe there is need for others' thoughts where your most penetrating intelligence serves you so well, whose hand I kiss in supplication. Farewell.

Ostellato 8 June 1503

GAZING these past days into my crystal, of which we spoke during the last evening I paid my respects to your Ladyship, I have read therein, glowing at its centre, these lines I now send to you inscribed upon this paper.† It would be the sweetest consolation to me and more prized than any treasure if in exchange your Ladyship might permit me to see some thing that she may have read in hers. And yet I cannot be sure that I may hope as much, when I recall that the day before yesterday you still kept silent regarding those things of which you had proposed to speak with me. I kiss your Ladyship's hand.

Ostellato   19 June 1503

† The sonnet, *Poi ch' ogni ardir*

*M*ESSER PIETRO mio. Concerning the desire you have to hear from me regarding the counterpart of your or our crystal as it may rightly be reputed and termed, I cannot think what else to say or imagine save that it has an extreme affinity of which the like perhaps has never been equalled in any age. And may this suffice. And let it be a gospel everlasting.

This henceforth shall be my name   f.f.

Ferrara 24 June 1503

Poi ch'ogni ardir mi circonscrisse Amore
Quel dì, ch'io posi nel suo regno il piede,
Tanto ch'altrui, non pur chieder mercede,
Ma scoprir sol non oso il mio dolore,
Avess'io almen d'un bel cristallo il core,
Che, quel ch'i' taccio & Madonna non vede
De l'interno mio mal, senza altra fede
A' suoi begli occhi tralucesse fore;
Ch'io spererei de la pietate ancora
Veder tinta la neve di quel volto,
Che 'l mio sì spesso bagna & discolora.
Or che questo non ho, quello m'è tolto,
Temo non voglia il mio Signor, ch'io mora:
La medicina è poca, il languir molto.

Since Love forbade my zeal while she was near
The first day I set foot in His domain,
Whence each cry for her mercy I restrain
And dare not let my wretchedness appear,
Would that I had a heart as crystal clear,
Then what I hide, nor she can ascertain,
Without more proof of my least inward pain
Would shine for her fair eyes in faith sincere;
I should yet hope to see that face divine
Tinged with pity that now is white as snow,
And much has moistened and discoloured mine.
My heart's no glass, and this I must forego,
And fear my Lord would wish to see me pine,
The remedy fail, the affliction grow.

*N*OW *is my crystal more precious to me than all the pearls of the Indian seas, and surely you have acted most mercifully in granting parity such as you have given it, and such company. God knows no human thing could be so dear to me as this certainty, and you too shall know it one day, if you do not yet. Nor is there anything about like cases which I have ever read, howsoever great and noble and wondrous, that I do not desire to equal at some time – and the spirit will not fail me while there is proof of that mercy which alone will always be at the centre of my crystal at every turn, on every occasion, at every hour. Since I last wrote to your Ladyship I have composed three sonnets upon the loveliest and most gracious dream I had a night or two ago; but being still poorly elaborated I reserve the right to send them to you another day together with some other verses for inclusion among your papers, as Eu. Jo.† asked me to do on your account. As soon as Messer Ercole has departed for Venice I shall come to pay homage to your Ladyship, whose hand I kiss in gratitude and to whom I commend my crystal.*

(Ostellato 24 June) 1503

† unidentified

YOUR *vexations distress me hardly less perhaps than they do you, and it could not be otherwise, for so it was and is decreed by my destiny and by the great debt of gratitude I owe to you, and ever shall. But apart from sharing your distress other things trouble me, and one of these is that I think you may be saddened at being unable to gladden my heart by your dear presence as often as perhaps you might have done, had your own not been burdened by these present cares. If this is so, then I would ask you to reflect that a thought resolved to last a lifetime cannot in any way be affected by a few days' distress, assuming this to be real distress, which can scarcely be the case if despite all your distressfulness you have not changed. I had and have and hope always to have that which I wanted and want and shall want without end, and am content with it. If you now start to feel concern for me on this account, I shall believe you are not kept content by having from me what I believe I have from you, and keeps me content.*

(Ostellato late June) 1503

Se 'l viver men che pria m'è duro e vile,
Né più d'Amor mi pento esser suggetto,
Né son di duol, come io solea, ricetto,
Tutto questo è tuo don, sogno gentile.
Madonna più che mai tranquilla, umile,
Con tai parole e 'n sì cortese affetto
Mi si mostrava, e tanto altro diletto,
ch'asseguir no 'l poria lingua né stile.
— Perché — dicea — la tua vita consume?
Perché pur del Signor nostro ti lagni?
Frena i lamenti omai, frena 'l dolore. —
E più cose altre; quando il primo lume
Del giorno sparse i miei dolci guadagni,
Aperti gli occhi e traviato il core

If this dire harsh life seems less extreme
And I protest no more against Love's reign,
Nor feel, as once, I harbour too much pain,
All is a gift from you, most noble dream.
More calm or meek my Lady could not seem,
Such were her words, her tender care so plain
In each delight the vision did contain,
No tongue or pen is equal to the theme.
'But why,' said she, 'thus wear your life away?
If one Lord rules us both, why so distressed?
Stay your complaints now, stay these tears you shed —'
And so much more beside; when the first ray
Of daylight stole the fortune I possessed
And I lay open-eyed, with heart misled.

*T*ODAY I would have come to pay tribute to your Ladyship, as was
my obligation or my desire – I know not which the more, for both were
vast and infinite – had it not been that the other night I woke with
such pain in my neck that now I can only move it if I turn my entire body,
and that with difficulty, and consequently it gives me no little annoyance.
I believe it was a bad strain, and certainly it was very bad of it to choose to
assail me at this time. But these past hours it has begun to perceive its error
and appears to be relenting and preparing to be gone; and no sooner is this
accomplished than I shall straightway come to your Ladyship, which will,
I deem, be within two days. And should it defer its departure longer I shall
come in any case, as I have no desire to follow this neckache with heartache,
which is wont to be much more serious – although I fear I am already
affected, seeing that I have delayed more than I should wish my coming to
kiss your hand. Accordingly I shall come quickly whatever happens, if only
to cure myself of this second malady. Here the heat is unusually intense and
for my part I have never felt it stronger – I seem to be all aflame and turned
to fire. I do not know whether you feel it to the same degree. In no wise, I
must suppose, for where you are there is more shade than I have here, nor
can I forget that by their nature women feel the heat less than men are wont
to do. Craving your favour I kiss your Ladyship's hand, and beg my dear
Madonna Lisabetta† to say one prayer for me to her saintly mistress.

Ostellato 29 June 1503

† Lisabetta da Siena, her lady-in-waiting

I REJOICE that each day to increase my fire you cunningly devise some fresh incitement, such as that which encircled your glowing brow today. If you do such things because, feeling some little warmth yourself, you wish to see another burn, I shall not deny that for each spark of yours untold Etnas are raging in my breast. And if you do so because it is natural for you to relish another's suffering, who in all justice could blame me if he but knew the reasons for my ardour? Truly I can do no sin if I put my faith in such a gospel and in so many miracles. Let Love wreak just revenge for me, if upon your brow you are not the same as in your heart.

Ferrara 14 July 1503

I AM leaving, oh my dearest life, and yet I do not leave and never shall. If likewise you who stay were not to stay, I dare not speak for you, but truly 'Ah, of all who love none more blest than I!' And what sweeter miracle could be wrought than this: to live in another and die in oneself? And oh, how truthfully I can swear I live in you! All this night, whether in dreams or lying awake, all this long night I was with you, and so far as this mortal condition can vouchsafe I hope it will be the same every night of my life. Do not, I entreat your Ladyship, disdain to attend most kindly and sweetly to that part of me which remains with you, and sometimes speak of it with my dear and saintly Lisabetta, in whose prayers I ask to be remembered. They say each has a good angel who prays for him, and I pray to that angel† who can pray for me that he will pray f.f. for that which he knows will profit me. All I know is that faith as pure and as constant as mine deserves the favour of your goodness. And were I an angel, as he is, I should be consumed with great pity for any man who loved as much as I. My heart kisses your Ladyship's hand which so soon I shall come to kiss with these lips that are forever forming your name – or rather with this very soul which even now is telling me that at that instant it will want to leap to my lips, and so take sweet revenge for its sweet wound.

Ferrara 18 July 1503

† Angela Borgia?

NOT because I am able to tell you what tender bitterness enfolds me at this parting do I write to you, light of my life, but only to entreat you to cherish yourself most dearly, and, lest my life perish, also your health, which would seem to be a little affected. That line which you had in part written upon my heart is now wholly engraved deep within, and it will admit nothing but the thought of you, so well have you deserved it. Alas, now I must depart. I kiss that tender hand which has slain me.

Ferrara 18 July 1503

WITH greatest reverence I have this very moment received your letter, sweet as everything which comes from you, and so full of that honey which can be gathered alone from the flower of your words, and nowhere else. I thank you for the news of your recovery from the two bouts of tertian fever, although I had heard no mention of any such tertian. And most fortunate was that for me, for if I had heard of it I should have been racked by it perpetually. All I was informed of was the favour you extended to my good Messer Lodovico †, deeply inflamed by your Lady-ship's surpassing qualities, indeed all afire. I thank you also for the dear things you say, and acknowledge that no words of mine can express the debt I owe you. As for my Asolani, I am deeply envious of it for many reasons. I never dared hope to be granted such happiness. At the most timely moment it came into your hands. Messer Lodovico writes to me saying that he feels there is no need for it to be brought out and read by all the world in order to gain glory, for more than it enjoys already could never come its way; and he speaks the truth. Well, I must try to give thought to something else that may reach you as this has done, in order that the felicity which cannot be mine may at least befall my writings. Farewell.

Ostellato 24 July 1503

† Lodovico Ariosto

*L*ONG *ago I took up this pen to thank your Ladyship for the most noble and gracious service you performed with your healing visit yesterday, when you deigned to come to my house and to my very bedside to see me and comfort me and stay a long while with me. But I do not know how to begin to thank you, I believe because the gratitude I owe you is so infinite that words, being finite, can add nothing. For the truth is your visit has rid me of all the faintness of fever I had, indeed has altogether dispelled every trace of my grievous illness, quite as if some celestial being had been sent down from above to cure me, and that vision alone and the merest pressure upon my wrist had been enough to bring back all the health I had before. But to this you appended those dear sweet words so full of love and joy and the very quick of sympathy. Accordingly I shall treasure the memory of this debt along with those others I have stored in my mind, which being of its own nature infinite can accommodate every infinite thing. I think I shall be up tomorrow. Meantime I commend myself to your Ladyship's good graces and kiss that hand sweeter than which was never kissed by man. I do not say lovelier, for lovelier could not be.*

Ferrara   12 August 1503

*I*N truth I called upon your Ladyship yesterday partly for the purpose of informing you what grief and concern your misfortune causes me, and in part to offer what comfort I could and urge you to compose yourself since I had heard how you were afflicted with sorrow beyond measure. But I was quite unable to accomplish either purpose, for as soon as I saw you lying there in that darkened room and in that black gown, so tearful and disconsolate, my feelings overwhelmed me and for a long time I stood there unable to utter a word, not knowing even what to say. And more in need of solace myself than able to proffer any, my spirit in turmoil at the pity of that spectacle, tongue-tied and stammering I withdrew, as you saw, or might have seen. If it be this befell me because you have no need of either my grief or my comfort, since being aware of my faith and devotion you know already how I must share your grief and you can take comfort within yourself by drawing on your infinite wisdom with need of nothing from without, then I shall be less anxious for myself and my poor powers which deserted me at that time. If, however, you would have me offer some adequate expression of my thoughts and feelings, then as for my grief there is no doubt that Fortune could have found no surer way of rendering me more sorrowful and grief-stricken than by giving you cause to grieve and sorrow, nor could any shaft of hers have pierced my soul as deep as that which flew to wound me bathed in your tears. And as for what comfort I would offer, I know not what else to say but to ask you to recall that Time soothes and lessens all our tribulations, and it would more become you, from whom all expect a most rare self-possession in view of the daily proofs you have given of your valour on every occasion and at every misadventure, not to delay such time but rather to prepare for it resolutely. Furthermore, although you have now lost your very great father, greater than whom Fortune herself could have granted you none, this is not the first blow which you have suffered at the hands of your cruel and malevolent destiny. Indeed your spirit ought by now to be inured to shocks of fate, so many and so bitter have you already suf-

fered. And what is more, you would do well not to allow anyone to assume, as some might be led to infer in present circumstances, that you bewail not so much your loss but what may betide your present fortunes. However, it may be I lack prudence in writing such things to you, and therefore I shall close, adding but one thing more. In serving you I should naturally much rather know you to be happy and content, indeed my supremest happiness would be to see you happy always and all ways; nevertheless I promise and swear to you that not only do these adverse events in no way alter or cool these warm and constant thoughts of mine, but they do yet further fire my resolve to serve you each day, so that the more you observe Fortune's face grow sombre the more my steadfast diamond glows. Farewell.

Ostellato   22 August 1503

I DO not write this to your Ladyship because I would crave the least favour of your mercy (the bridle of my desires I now relinquish to the hands of chance since when I hold the reins they do not take the path I wish), but only to assure you of two things. Firstly, that I would not rather have come by some great treasure than hear what I heard from you yesterday, although – as our sworn affinity deserved – you might well have let me know it earlier. And secondly, that as long as there is life in me my cruel fate will never prevent the fire in which f.f. and my destiny have placed me from being the highest and brightest blaze that in our time ever set a lover's heart alight. It will soar by virtue of the place where it burns, bright with the intensity of its own flame, and one day it will be a beacon to all the world. The state of grace to which in your great charity you have raised me, whether extended still or now withheld, is such honour that no other woman could ever again enter my thoughts, for none could rival you in excellence; and were I even to lose my life in thus consigning myself to the flames for the third time it would still be well with me, since all third things being so perilous in the undertaking are wont to enjoy a special benediction. Not chance nor fortune, not place nor time, not the world entire, and not even you, can alter this resolve. Now I feel that I could write so many things to you for which I could not find words yesterday, when you could see how 'pure love inflamed | Ties the tongue and bears the spirit away.' And if it happens that you fail to perceive how I am from the way I live, or you cannot read my feelings in my eyes and upon my countenance, what use may I suppose you could have for letters? If the future holds little happiness in store for me, such may be the will of heaven so that I may bear witness to a deep faith and a rare spirit. Now think me false as much as you will, believe the truth as little as you please, but like it or not the day shall come when you must acknowledge how far you judged me wrong. There are times I fear this is not so much how others would have you believe, it is your very own opinion. And if this be so, then I hope that the motto I read among your papers a few

days ago will prove to be true : quien quiere matar perro ravia le levanta †.
*Make a merry blaze of all my other letters, and this alone I beg you deign
to keep as pledge for what I write. And so it shall be that for as many years
to come as we have lived you shall be free to consult it to your satisfaction,
and to my honour. In supplication I kiss your hand.*

(Ostellato) 5 October 1503

† He who would kill a dog must himself work up a rage

EIGHT days have passed since I parted from f.f., and already it is as though I had been eight years away from her, although I can avow that not one hour has passed without her memory which has become such a close companion to my thoughts that now more than ever is it the food and sustenance of my soul; and if it should endure like this a few days more, as seems it must, I truly believe it will in every way have assumed the office of my soul, and I shall then live and thrive on the memory of her as do other men upon their souls, and I shall have no life but in this single thought. Let the God who so decrees do as he will, so long as in exchange I may have as much a part of her as shall suffice to prove the gospel of our affinity is founded on true prophecy. Often I find myself recalling, and with what ease, certain words spoken to me, some on the balcony with the moon as witness, others at that window I shall always look upon so gladly, with all the many endearing and gracious acts I have seen my gentle lady perform – for all are dancing about my heart with a tenderness so wondrous that they inflame me with a strong desire to beg her to test the quality of my love. For I shall never rest content until I am certain she knows what she is able to enact in me and how great and strong is the fire that her great worth has kindled in my breast. The flame of true love is a mighty force, and most of all when two equally matched wills in two exalted minds contend to see which loves the most, each striving to give yet more vital proof. But sometimes far greater than a love which can be freely manifest is the flame of a love which may not reveal itself however deeply it might desire. I have striven to render into Tuscan your Crió el ciel y el mundo Dios† *but can discover no means to convey the same sentiment to my satisfaction in this tongue, least of all in the form of a copla and with similar words. Nevertheless I enclose a sonnet which was begun with the intention of treating the same theme and then took a different turn because it could not hold to the same path and still hold true to my ultimate design, whereof I must and do desire to write always in the highest terms. I hear that you are well, though of your being indisposed on the day I took my leave I shall say no more. It would be the greatest delight for me to see just two lines in f.f.'s hand, yet I dare not ask so much. May your Ladyship beseech her to perform whatever you feel is best for me. With my heart I kiss your Ladyship's hand, since I cannot with my lips.*

(Venice) 18 October 1503

† unidentified Spanish *copla* which inspired the accompanying sonnet, *L'alta cagion*

L'alta cagion, che da principio diede
A le cose create ordine e stato,
Dispose ch'io v'amassi e dielmi in fato,
Per far di sé col mondo exempio e fede.
Che sì come virtù da lei procede,
Che 'l tempra e regge, e come è sol beato
A cui per grazia il contemplarla è dato,
Et essa è d'ogni affanno ampia mercede,
Così 'l sostegno mio da voi mi vene
Od in atti cortesi od in parole,
E sol felice son, quand'io vi miro.
Né maggior guiderdon de le mie pene
Posso aver di voi stessa, ond'io mi giro
Pur sempre a voi, come elitropio al sole

The supreme cause which at the start did give
Things created their measure and their state
Willed me to love you and accept my fate
To manifest the faith whereby we live.
As virtues from that principle derive,
Ruler, moderator, sole joy innate
Whose face the fortunate may contemplate
Who seeking peace by grace abounding strive,
Yours is the radiance which makes me burn,
And growing with each act and gracious word
My joy in seeing you is never done.
Nor for my restlessness is there reward
Higher than yourself, wherefore I turn
To you, as heliotrope looks to the sun.

*S*UCH *are worldly cares: if they be many they commonly become so enmeshed that when we mean to take up but one we find we have hold of a great number, as though they formed a chain to whose first ring or link a second were joined, and to that a third, and so on and on without let or break. So much have I learned on this occasion, when, after coming here to see to a matter requiring no more than two days' attention, I have had to attend to numberless others which quite against my wishes the first of necessity brought in its train. But what gave me most concern was finding my father's life at grave risk after a fall, in which condition I could not humanly have left him before today; but now he is himself again and gives no cause for worry, though there was much before. Tomorrow I shall be in Venice and after two days there, as I promised your Ladyship, I shall come back to see once more my own dear half without whom I am not merely incomplete but nothing at all, she being not simply one half of me but everything I am and can ever hope to be. And there could be no sweeter fate for me on earth, nor could I win anything more precious than to lose myself like this, living the rest of my life in one thought alone, which, if in two hearts one and the same purpose thrives, and one single fire, may endure as long as those hearts wish, no matter what the heavens conspire. And this they can all the more readily accomplish because strangers' eyes are unable to discern their thoughts and no human power can bar the road they take, since they come and go unseen. Beseeching your favour I kiss your hand, and send my respects to my dear Madonna Lisabetta.*

Noniano 25 October 1503

Pietro to Lucrezia (in Medelana)   XVIII

IF I have come here without your Ladyship's leave it is because I thought I should be gone again at once. But now, because at Ostellato, as I told you, there are no provisions on account of the visit of his Lordship Don Alfonso's court, and because the time has come for me to recall that this summer I promised you I should spend the winter in Ferrara, I shall not move from here, more especially because, assuming the course of the plague improves, as seems to be the case, it will not be many days before your Ladyship returns here too; not to mention that no sooner do I speak of departure than Messer Ercole threatens to keep me here whether I will or no. Ah well, I shall remain here respectfully and unless you refuse all who desire to see you I shall call to pay my homage from time to time. And this I would wish to be able to do as often as I desire, or desire to do no less seldom than I am able. Commending myself to your good graces I kiss your hand.

Ferrara 2 November 1503

Da quella che nel cor scolpita porto
Vi ritrasse il pittore,
Mentre per gli occhi fore,
Qual sète dentro agevolmente ha scorto.

Engraved within my heart a fair form lies,
In your likeness here portrayed;
The shrewd master's hand betrayed
Its secret life by gazing in your eyes.

AND now I too have to exchange my careworn grey for dismal black. The auguries I took, and likewise those of your Ladyship, contained a prediction that was all too true. Carlo, my dear and only brother, my life's sole support and delight, has departed to heaven with the best part of my heart. On reaching here I found not only that he was dead but buried too, and thus has been fulfilled that Bible verse which before leaving you I chanced upon while seeking some augury of what might lie in store: 'And he slept with his fathers, and they buried him in the city of David.'† Oh, accursed and barbarous evil destiny! Woe is me, that you could not rest content with the many treacherous and grievous injuries I have suffered from your hand at every step along life's way, since you still had to inflict this further wound, deeper and more harrowing than which you could not have dealt without slaying me; for you have seen fit to take from me in the very flower of his manhood, oh harsh and cruel gods, the one person whose efforts on my behalf rendered hardships easier to bear and happier times, though few have been my lot, a little sweeter! I am sending for my books that I left in Ferrara, and shall not move from here for a while so that at least during these days my elderly and grieving father need not remain bereft of all light, for there is little doubt he needs my comfort. Of my return I shall say no more than that I know not what to say. But this much I can say to you in all truth, and you must believe me, that here and wherever else I may be, disconsolate or cheered, I shall always be that faithful Heliotrope to whom you alone and for ever remain the sun. I kiss your Ladyship's hand, and if I may be of assistance to you in any way I beg you with all my power not to disdain to remember I am your servant; for I shall be that much less unhappy the more you deign to command me. Farewell.

Venice 5 January 1504

† 2 Chronicles IX, v. 31

THE tears which you write you could not withstrain when reading in my letter of the death of my dearly loved brother Messer Carlo have been the sweetest balm for me in my sorrow, if anything can seem sweet to me at such a time. To learn that you felt such tender friendship for me in my bereavement exceeds far more than I can say all condolences I have received in letters or in other ways upon this my most hard and bitter blow. Accordingly I offer your Ladyship my deepest thanks, and feel more than ever beholden to you now that I have fallen upon such ill-fortune and profound unhappiness, my hopes and quietude of life in ruins. And as much as I can, with the patience you urge upon me, I shall endeavour to bear the burden of my misfortune, heavy though it is, encouraged by the example of your Ladyship's own fortitude in her adversities. And kiss your hand.

Venice 22 January 1504

*T*HERE *was no need for your Ladyship to make apologies for not having written to me very often, for as long as you recall that I am your servant I ask no more, and never shall. From your Majordomo I have gathered how you had intended coming here during Lent and that you now believe it will be Ascensiontide. The former will grieve me less should the latter come to pass. I shall not presume to entreat your Ladyship to make it so, for it is not for me to offer up so high a prayer. However, should you deign to come you will, I believe, discover diversion and delight in plenty, but far greater shall be mine at your coming. All who visit us from Ferrara tell me how you are lovelier now than ever before, wherein I rejoice with you. I would dearly pray to heaven that with every day that passes it might increase your beauty, though I truly believe nothing can add to it. Besides, if that which you already possess so manifestly enslaves all who but once set eyes upon you, what might ensue if you could be, and were, still lovelier than you are now? I have had many most agreeable discussions with your Majordomo and since his arrival am half-way recovered from my recent troubles. One scarce dares think how it will be if your Ladyship should come here too, whose hand I kiss in supplication.*

Venice 28 March 1504

MESSER *Pietro mio. To my singular delight and solace I have received and read a letter from you and have taken note of what you write to me. I thank you most profusely, although on the other hand I was grieved to learn in this same letter of yours that you feel so discontented at this time also because I know it is your desire to obtain two lines from the hand of f.f. and she for many good reasons has not been able to comply with this petition despite the anxiety she has to please and content you. Nonetheless I am glad in her stead to make amends with these few lines in my own hand persuaded as I am that they will bring you some little consolation and peace of mind; wherefore I beg you all I can to consider her excused in this for my sake and to accept her goodwill towards you which I can testify is ever most bent upon your gratification and service, whereunto it may please you no doubt to be good witness.*

Wishing to gratify you
Lucretia Estense de Borgia

Ferrara 29 March (1504)

I ACCEPT every excuse which you offer on f.f.'s behalf; and all those reasons, which you say are many, for her not writing to me despite her desire to gratify me have been constantly before my eyes and I picture them to myself even while asking you for two lines from her hand. And yet I cannot help wishing for her letters now that seeing her and speaking with her, formerly two such strong and cherished pillars sustaining my life, have been dislodged and taken from me. The third still stands and always shall, for nothing save that which is the extreme end of all things could ever deprive me of it: I mean the thought, the memory, of her who encircles my heart each day, each night, every hour, wheresoever I am, whatever my condition. But if at times this thought, since it burns, perchance must crave a little relief, you should excuse it, and f.f. will also perform an act of great mercy if she will bear it in mind. You can imagine how much delight her letters would give me always if I tell you that this single apology from you for her silence has consoled me so greatly that I hope to live with this sustenance a few days more. Accordingly I extend to you all thanks I can, and not wishing to trouble you with further reading during these holy days shall end now, without end commending myself to your good graces, and her mercy.

Venice Good Friday, 5 April 1504

† Lisabetta da Siena, Lucrezia's lady-in-waiting, here a screen for her mistress

*I*T was my desire, and no less my duty, to come with Messer Ercole to visit you, and it would have been well for me, indeed essential, to secure this comfort for my spirit which for a good while now has been weighed down with cares and melancholy thoughts. But a recent and unexpected indisposition, due more to my state of mind than any other cause, will not even permit me to write to you as I should desire, let alone think of leaving here. Wherefore your Ladyship will, I trust, forgive me if I send you these few paltry lines when I should be sending many and with rich retinue. Meantime I shall console myself with the hope that I can come to kiss your hand as soon as I am up, if heaven will assist me. For the many greetings which both Messer Ercole and Messer Guido† and also your Majordomo have conveyed to me on your Ladyship's behalf, I thank your sweet humanity as far as I am able, and commending myself to your kind favour, kiss your hand. Farewell.

Venice 22 May 1504

† Guido Strozzi, Ercole's younger brother

ALTHOUGH I have legitimate cause for not writing to you, in appreciation of the goodwill you have shown me, and being informed of your indisposition which gives me much concern, I felt it would be discourteous of me not to let you know of this in these few lines: both to satisfy the desire you have that the letter should be in my hand and to express my obligation to you. It only remains for me to beg you all I can to promise to take good care of your health from now on; and you may trust the bearer of this as you would myself.

f.f.

(Ferrara late May 1504)

I THANK your Ladyship infinitely for the good wishes which Messer Ercole Pio conveyed to me in your name, and I need hardly say how fortunate I count myself since your Ladyship, knowing to what extent I am her servant, may esteem this for herself. For some time I have been about to come to pay tribute to your Ladyship, but day after day have been thwarted by my duties and have delayed until now, and now I hear your Ladyship has gone to Modena. Therefore I have changed my plan, resolving to go to a little villa of mine for two months so that I may finish those things which I began for you. If during this period you chance to find your ears are ringing it will be because I am communing with all those dark things and horrors and tears of yours, or else writing pages about you that will still be read a century after we are gone; and this, if it be owing to no perfection they may have, shall be due to the high renown of your name which they bear before them, and which of itself is companion to eternity.

Venice 25 July 1504

VINCENZO and I send your Ladyship boundless thanks for the kindness you showed in sending Antonio's capitolo †, truly enchanting and admirable in every way and which we greatly enjoyed, nor are we surprised that equally it delighted you. I did not ask Messer Ercole to convey a letter to your Ladyship since he came and went, as they say, as a bolt of lightning, and we scarcely saw him. I fear I have not written to your Ladyship for many days, having spent some weeks in my Paduan villa, although I trust you will not say that this has made a villein of me seeing that I was at liberty to give you news of myself and of country life and other places. On your behalf Messer Ercole urged me many times to bring out the Asolani, *though even once would have been unnecessary as I have not yet forgotten how great is my obligation to you, neither could it ever be forgotten. However, certain very important duties of mine have prevented me from satisfying until today my supreme desire always to obey your Ladyship. Now, as I informed Messer Ercole, I have put the finishing touches to it and if all were up to me it could come out tomorrow as I have no need to look it over further. The one thing which could persuade me not to part with it a few days more, or even months, is known to Messer Ercole, as I have spoken to him about it. And so you may see how that same ill-fate which has sorely tried me on so many other occasions, and which has made me appear to be other than I truly am, has not abandoned me yet. However I am long past paying much heed to it, for now I see that everything I held dear and precious which could be taken from me it has taken, so that all I am left with is my life, which I do not doubt it would have taken altogether with everything else were life still as precious and dear to me as it once was. But now, perceiving how I chide and despise it, fate lets me keep it, barely against my will. During these days I have received a letter from Monsignor Villaruel in Valencia, and many kind words on the part of Madonna Giovanna. He writes, among other things, asking me to let him know that all fares well with you, which I have done. The bearer of this letter, Messer*

Alfonso Ariosto, comes to you deeply desiring to render you homage and make your acquaintance, already afire with the flame that the rays of your great qualities have kindled in his breast, having heard them praised so many times. And talking with him yesterday of like matters I whiled away an hour most enchantingly, or gained it rather, since all others are spent or squandered to no purpose. He merits your kind favour on this account alone, and also because he is in truth a most civil and judicious young gentleman, as deserving as could be wished. I kiss your Ladyship's hand, as does also Messer Vincenzo.

Venice 22 September 1504

† poem by Antonio Tebaldeo forwarded to Bembo and his Venetian friend, Vincenzo Quirino

I HAD *planned to come and call upon your Ladyship in these days before returning home, and accordingly now having visited Bergamo and Brescia I wanted to journey on to Mantua and thence to Ferrara in order to slake in part my year-long thirst, as the bearer of this, Messer Alfonso Ariosto, knows right well, and with whom I settled on this course almost a month ago. But upon arriving here we heard that the Lord Duke, your father-in-law, had either departed this life or else was close to such a pass, and that the Marquess and Marchesa† had gone to Ferrara upon receiving the news. This has caused me to change my mind since it did not seem to be a time in which I should be able to pay my respects to you as unhurriedly as I should desire, and therefore on Messer Alfonso's advice I have deferred my coming to Ferrara until after Carnival. Every deferment which I find I am compelled to make distresses me deeply, especially when I consider that your Ladyship may think me a most cold and faint-hearted slave of hers if I can endure to live so long without seeing her. But your Ladyship will, I trust, excuse me for the reasons I have given, and after the holiday I shall assuredly come and make my obeisance to you. I would further urge and beseech your Ladyship kindly to take the trouble to prevail most earnestly upon Messer Ercole to send the package necessary for the printing of the Asolani, as he promised he would. Because when I am in Venice, which will be some four to six days hence, I intend to send it forth to try its fortune. Your Ladyship would do me a most singular favour if she would see to it that Messer Ercole does so, and he can so very easily and at no trouble to himself. I kiss the hand of your most illustrious Ladyship.*

Verona 8 October 1504

† The Duke's daughter, Isabella d'Este, wife of the Marquess of Mantua

*I*KNOW *I merit no small rebuke for not writing to your Ladyship for many days, and yet I presume to beg you to forgive me since I know that your humanity and courtesy are boundless, and also because the truth is that day after day I have been on the point of leaving to come and pay homage to you, and in this expectation have delayed writing much longer than I need have done. Cursed be the numberless occupations of men that will not let them live as they would wish, as surely I do not, and doubt I ever shall at any time unless I sever all the chains that bind me by seizing the desperate blade which my unhappiness so often pictures to my eyes. I had very little opportunity to enjoy Messer Ercole's company these days since I spent a great part of my time in Padua. And now I write to your Ladyship amidst many distractions. May your Ladyship be pleased to remember I am still her slave, and if deprived of her healing presence, 'Woes have I many yet none ails me so.' Commending myself to your good graces I kiss that hand which Messer Ercole will kiss for me. As ever deeply desiring to hear that all happiness is yours.*

Venice 10 November 1504

*A*S long as I have lived I cannot recall ever receiving a letter as gratify-ing as that which your Ladyship gave me upon my departure and in which you proved to me that I abide in your favour. Though it is true that I have had a number of indications before now, this assurance written in your own hand brings me boundless joy and satisfaction, and I offer you all the thanks which I, having no good but you, am bound to render for a gift so precious. And in reply, if your Ladyship says that I did well in bring-ing some solace to your anguish with my letter and that you were long awaiting it, I say you must know the first hour I saw you that you pene-trated my mind to such a degree that never afterwards have you been able to quit it through any cause. And if I said nothing of this to you for a long time it was because my accursed ill-fortune, never more powerful than when opposing all my deepest desires, decreed it so, for I had no choice but to con-fine the flames of my love wholly within my afflicted burning heart. And although this same ill-fortune is more than ever arrayed against me now, yet have I no fear, for it could never make me so afraid that I could cease to love you and not count you the one dear mistress of my self and my life, ever serving you with the purest and warmest loyalty that a valiant and steadfast lover can offer the woman he loves and honours above all things human. I do beseech you never to alter and never to lose heart in this love, though there are so many things which obstruct and oppose our desires, as you can see, but endeavour rather to be ever more deeply inflamed with love the more arduous you see your resolve become. And I would ask you to reflect that anyone can love when all fares well and all seems well-disposed, but if instead there are for ever a thousand harsh and conflicting things, a thousand separations, a thousand watchmen, a thousand barriers and a thousand walls, then not all can love, and if able to they may not so desire,

† Probably Nicola Trotti, lady-in-waiting, here a screen for Lucrezia

or if they desire they do not persevere; and by this token it is rendered a much rarer thing, and being rare it is possessed of still greater beauty in itself, is more magnanimous and more admirable, and a far finer ambition, the mark of a great and exalted heart. For however much more I would desire peace rather than tribulation for our flames this does not mean that at heart I do not account myself happy when I consider upon what summit my thoughts are set, that in spite of ill-fortune I love you and that nothing can take this from me; and I fancy, if there be likewise nothing that can make you not love me, in the end the day must come when we two shall triumph and vanquish ill-fortune, so long as we do not let it overwhelm and defeat us in the interval. And when that day comes it will be so lovely and precious for us to recall that we were staunch and constant lovers, and it will seem to us that we are only truly happy because we share this memory, since battles long and hard-fought make the victory all the greater and more cherished. And since your Ladyship tells me that you do not desire to live your life except to serve me, I say to you that not only from now on shall I too desire and seek solely to live my life for your service, but I shall at no time hesitate to place it at risk or sacrifice it to do your bidding. And seeing that whatever happens it is always the case that one must die, and ten or twenty years more or less cannot alter the truth that once and for all time we must bid this sky farewell, far sweeter would it be for me to die today serving and pleasing you than to live a great deal longer denied your favour. Therefore if your Ladyship feels that I am worthy of any undertaking which might please you, I beseech you without the least regard for my life to entrust me with it. Above all I beg you to take care that no one may know or discover your true thoughts lest the paths which lead to our love become even more restricted and thwarted than they are at present. Do not trust anyone, no matter whom, until I come to you, which in any case will be soon after Easter, if I am still alive. The man who brings you this, a most trustworthy friend of mine, is journeying on at once to Carpi and will return to hear whether there is any-

thing your Ladyship wishes to command me. In the meantime you may deign to write a reply to this, and give it to him in utmost secrecy, for it will be in safe keeping. Indeed I beseech you so to do, for since we can talk so little face to face please speak at length with me in letters and let me know what life you lead, and what thoughts are yours and in whom you confide, which things torment you and which console. And take good care not to be seen writing, because I know you are watched very closely. I shall come to Ferrara when Easter is past, as I told you, and shall go on to Rome for a month, or little more. Now I kiss your Ladyship's gentle hand by which my heart is bound, and more, if you will let me be so bold, I plant a kiss upon one of those prettiest and brightest and sweetest eyes of yours which have pierced me to the soul, first and lovely cause, though not the only one, of my ardour. Sometimes may it please you to recall that I think of nothing, esteem nothing, honour nothing, save you, and if I knew that I could fly with my departed spirit and be near you always I should desire no more to live. Nor shall I ever fear Fortune's onslaughts or what further harms she may devise if I know I dwell in your thoughts and in your Ladyship's love, for I desire no other happiness in this life but you, sweetest rest and haven for my storm-tossed soul. Out of love for me sometimes please deign to wear at night the enclosed Agnus Dei which I once used to wear upon my breast, if you cannot wear it in the day, so that your precious heart's dear abode, which I should gladly stake my life to kiss but once and long, may at least be touched by this roundel which for so long has touched the abode of mine. Farewell.

Venice 10 February 1505

The Letters

PART TWO
1505 to 1519

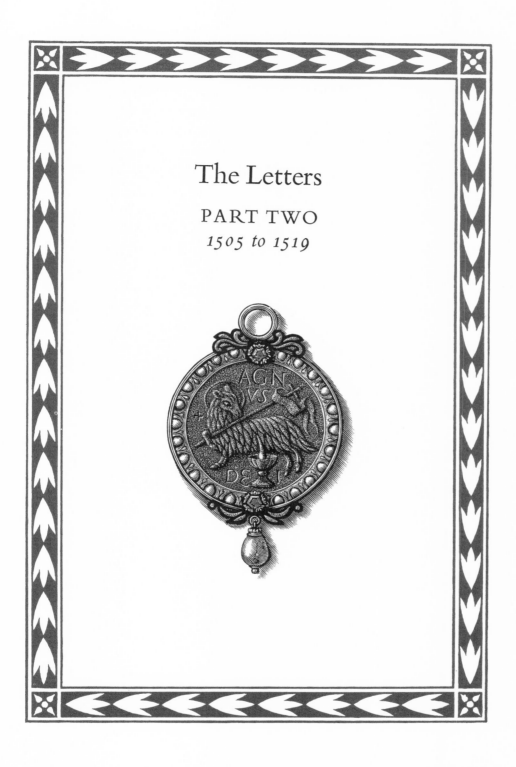

*I*T *afforded me infinite pleasure to receive in these days the public announcement of the happy birth of a male child to your Ladyship. Especially precious and cheering was it for me since I cannot tell you how anxiously it was awaited in view of the cruel disappointment and vain hopes of last year. Praised be heaven, for when the time is ripe 'to righteous prayers / His clemency shall lend an ear benign'. I am overjoyed on your Ladyship's behalf no more and no less than your own great happiness and the devotion and loyalty I bear you do deserve. And I pray to those same stars, which being perchance mindful no less of your merit than of the public good have now granted you an heir to such an illustrious State, that they may also cause this so dearly awaited son to wax worthy of so fine a mother and make you and the Lord Duke his father more abundantly content with their noble scion than all the happiest and most contented parents who ever lived. As for myself, who have long been a servant to your Ladyship and the Lord Duke, I shall henceforth be more happy in the knowledge that there is born one to whom in due time I shall be able to offer my homage and devotion, and as soon as I am granted an opportunity I shall come to see this sweet little new Lord of mine. Meantime I commend myself ever to your good graces, reverently kissing your beautiful and exquisite hand.*

Venice 23 September 1505

DEARLY would I wish to be adequate to all the thanks I feel are owed for the infinite courtesy you have shown in choosing to write to inform me of your most happy delivery. And although I was overjoyed to hear of it through the public proclamations, as you will have learned from my earlier letter, to receive it also as a personal gift and favour from you was so precious and welcome to me that nothing could have happened at this time to gratify and please me more, and not least because I feel it is a sign that I am still accounted your loyal servant. But seeing I am forced to acknowledge that my powers are too frail to thank you sufficiently I shall treasure this great debt in my memory, offering you once more my congratulations on this dear and so fondly desired delivery of such a sweet little baby boy, no less fortunate in being your child than heir to so fine and grand a State. I am glad too that both he and you are in good health, as you inform me, which makes both my joy and his happiness full and complete. I received your letter whilst journeying, being on my return from the countryside about Treviso where I spent a few days in most agreeable diversion, though not such as to be traded for those days in my good Messer Ercole's Ostellato which often still keeps house for that only part of me which can dwell there now. I kiss your hand, reverently begging you to deign to kiss just once that dear and tender little Lord of mine on my account.

Venice 30 September 1505

*T*ULLIO † *has at this very moment brought greetings from your Ladyship and given me your very kind letter. I am truly overjoyed whenever I see signs that your Ladyship still preserves some memory of me, her meanest servant, for I feel that this life no longer has anything so precious to offer me. For such tender consideration I offer your Ladyship not what thanks are due, for they are boundless, but all within my power. And would to heaven that some day I might be adequate to the task of convincing your Ladyship how much I am beholden to her, in order that my inadequacy might no more prey upon my mind, which has far more things locked within than it has ever been capable of manifesting. What sorrow I felt at the loss which your Ladyship sustained of her little son, and my Lord, I shall not say, since I would not increase your distress. Nevertheless I send you a forecast, which I had prepared for him here by a man skilled in this art as soon as I received notice of his birth, so that your Ladyship may discover some consolation in reflecting that we are truly in great part ruled by the stars. Commending myself to your good graces, reverently I kiss your hand.*

Venice 29 November 1505

† Bembo's man-servant

I AM at a loss to explain, most excellent Lady, how all those in the suite of the noble Lord Duke, your consort, were able to leave without my giving one of them a letter for your Ladyship, if only to thank you for the many affectionate greetings which were conveyed to me by almost everyone I spoke with who was here. But however it came to pass, due either to my many occupations or to my having trusted that Messer Pier Antonio Acciaiolo would not depart without contacting me since he had promised not to return to your Ladyship without bringing a letter of mine, I ask you in your kindness to forgive my error. I must further thank you for the pleasure which you desired me to know you felt on hearing of the position to which his Holiness has appointed me, and although I had no need of this proof of it to know your feelings I am nevertheless most grateful. I wish to assure your Ladyship that not merely this office but any other that I might ever receive, no matter how exalted or illustrious, could ever halt or divert me by so much as one single step from my long servitude to your Ladyship, more dear to me and precious than any dominion. I kiss your Ladyship's hand, without end commending myself to your favour.

Rome 11 May 1513

*T*HE *cares of my office, so many that they rob me of a moment's leisure, have been all the more irksome to me since I have been unable to pay tribute to your Ladyship by letter as frequently as my long and loyal devotion and service to you require. In consequence the thought torments me that your Ladyship may say that some little second good fortune may have obliterated from my memory the many, indeed infinite, obligations I bear to you. However, no sooner have I framed this thought than I fall to thinking that to imagine that the height of your Ladyship's mind could stoop so low as to misjudge a servant of such long standing on account of little diligence shown, were a poor thought indeed and deserving reprehension. And this second thought, tossing the other to the ground, remains on its feet to my great pleasure. And thus I live in the very certain hope that your Ladyship believes that no manner of good fortune that may come my way, not even were it to be more happy and prosperous than all other mortal honours, could ever suffice to banish from my mind the strong and steadfast and persistent fidelity pledged to your Ladyship many years ago, and so true is this that it is the greatest truth I know. And should there be need of a witness to it I could summon your Ladyship's faithful friend the Monsignor Treasurer.† He often talks of you with me, and sometimes it happens that I am with him when he receives a letter from your Ladyship which he prizes so highly that I find him never more gladdened by anything, and most of all when he sees that it is written all in your own hand. Ah well, I must confess to your Ladyship that in this matter I envy him no little, indeed much. And there are times when I would wish to be a Treasurer, and more. Nay, being even as I am I can take umbrage. And I declare that I shall not pen the breve of absolution for your Ladyship, which Messer Latino ‡ seeks to obtain, unless I first receive a letter from you entirely in your own hand. Then I shall see whether you care to be absolved or not. I kiss your Ladyship's hand, and reverently commend myself to your good graces, begging you to be pleased in person to commend me to the orisons of my most reverend mothers Sister Laura and Sister Afrosina.*

Rome 17 June 1513

† Bernardo Bibbiena   ‡ Latino Juvenale, Papal Nuncio

MESSER *Pietro mio carissimo. Since I know that when something is expected the expectation is a great part of the pleasure because the hope of possessing that thing kindles our desire, picturing it to us seldom as it is and more often far more beautiful than it is, I proposed to delay replying to your letter until today, so that while awaiting some beautiful reward for your very beautiful letter you might yourself be the cause of your own pleasure, being at once creditor and debtor. Furthermore, having confessed in two letters to the Monsignor Treasurer the debt I owe you, I think you might accept it as no small part of that which I can pay, and for the rest I do not think I can be held to account, because while you in your letter express with ease all you feel for me, I because I feel so much for you cannot do likewise, and hence consider myself absolved of my entire debt in virtue of this disability. But because it would not be proper for me to be both attorney and judge in my own case I humbly submit to the most solemn judgement of the aforesaid Monsignor Treasurer, infinitely commending myself to his Excellency and to you.*

Your Duchess of Ferrara

Ferrara 7 August (1513)

MESSER *Pietro mio. My Most Reverend Monsignor San Sixto†
has informed me how promptly and willingly you acted concerning
the dispatch of a certain breve which I desired to obtain. I thank
you all I can for everything and remain as indebted to you as such unceasing
loyal regard deserves and which shall be content to know it is repaid in
equal measure, therefore I shall not write any more for now, especially as I
do not feel so well at present.*

Your Duchess of Ferrara

3 March (1514)

† Cardinal Achilles de Grassis

I KISS *your Ladyship's hand, and leave it to the gallant Messer Latino, his Holiness's Nuncio, to offer my apologies for the long silence I have kept with you, and to render thanks for your gift and the beautiful little cap, and also to report a number of other things to you on my behalf. And I am glad of this because he will do it better than ever I could in writing, and also because in this way I avoid the need to make excuses, truly a diffi- cult task, as there are no mean reasons that I might give. I commend myself without end to your Ladyship's good graces and mercy. I know not which is better, to be great and a slave, or mean and free. This much I know: to be mean and a slave is the worst fate of all.*

Rome 27 September 1514

MESSER *Pietro mio cordialissimo. As I gathered from your letter and from Messer Latino's account to me there are many good reasons why you avoid making excuses, and I for no less good reasons will avoid accusations and choose to think your every act has an honourable motive, and am content that you have a little more respite for your leisure. I should be pleased if you would repay this by even more frequently commending me humbly at the feet of his Holiness reminding him of my most devoted service which ever increases as in his clemency his Beatitude never ceases to add to my numberless obligations which I can recompense in no way save in perpetual and most loyal service. For your and my, or rather my and your, most reverend Monsignor Santa Maria in Portico † I have nothing to add at present having charged Messer Latino to speak with him on his arrival, and he will also mention certain other things to you on my behalf, wherefore I shall write no more for now except to assure you once more of my continuing goodwill towards you.*

Your Duchess of Ferrara.

Ferrara 2 January (1515)

† Bernardo Bibbiena, by now elevated to Cardinal

ASIDE from that which, Messer Pietro mio, our good Messer Latino will report to you by word of mouth, for my greater satisfaction with these few words in my own hand I hereby testify to my unceasing good-will towards you, with promise to persevere firmly.

Your Duchess of Ferrara.

Ferrara (late 1515)

YOUR Ladyship well knows the nature of my destiny which forever grants me least what I desire most. I am unable to give myself the satisfaction of coming to pay you my respects as I had planned, and as you also sought me to do, since I am obliged to return with his Holiness to Florence. I trust your Highness will pardon me this misfortune though I cannot pardon my aforementioned destiny for it. Truly I hope without fail, before the end of Carnival, to be able to give myself the satisfaction of coming to Ferrara for three days, as the bearer of this, Messer Agostino Beazzano, a most worthy man and my devoted friend, will make clear to your Highness when he is with you, and I leave all to him. I kiss your Highness's hand in gratitude for the four lines in her hand. Ah, if only I could see every two months a scrap of paper on which you had written, how much more venturesome I should be! At all events I hope one day to end these demanding duties of mine and live a free man. And if my aforesaid destiny were only in the smallest way kind to me I should already have made good this desire. Humbly I commend myself without end to your Highness's good graces.

Bologna 18 December 1515

HAVING come to Bologna in connection with the Rhodes benefice in this city which I recently received, although it should have been mine years past, and being unable to proceed further owing to the brief time permitted me away from Rome, I wish with these few lines to pay my respects to your Ladyship, assuring her that I am still that devoted servant of hers which it is meet I should be and have ever been. And this no span of time nor change of fortune will ever alter, nor prevent my hoping that at some less busy time I may be able both to visit you and serve you. I kiss your Highness's hand and respectfully commend myself to her good graces.

Bologna 13 October 1517

*M*ESSER *Pietro mio. I have recently kept company with your own negligence in the past having been so late in replying to a letter from you which was especially welcome to me and for which I now thank you all I can and beg you to believe most firmly that just as every day I appreciate more your unceasing goodwill towards me so my obligation and goodwill to you increase and multiply. The more I consider that remedy for despair which that friend of yours once told you the more it pleases me and I find it as apt as ever.*